D1555320

Political Traditions in Foreign Policy Series
Kenneth W. Thompson, Editor

The values, traditions, and assumptions undergirding approaches to foreign policy are often crucial in determining the course of a nation's history. Yet, the interconnections between ideas and policy for landmark periods in our foreign relations remain largely unexamined. The intent of this series is to encourage a marriage between political theory and foreign policy. A secondary objective is to identify theorists with a continuing interest in political thought and international relations, both younger scholars and the small group of established thinkers. Only occasionally have scholarly centers and university presses sought to nurture studies in this area. In the 1950s and 1960s the University of Chicago Center for the Study of American Foreign Policy gave emphasis to such inquiries. Since then the subject has not been the focus of any major intellectual center. The Louisiana State University Press and the series editor, from a base at the Miller Center of Public Affairs at the University of Virginia, have organized this series to meet a need that has remained largely unfulfilled since the mid-1960s.

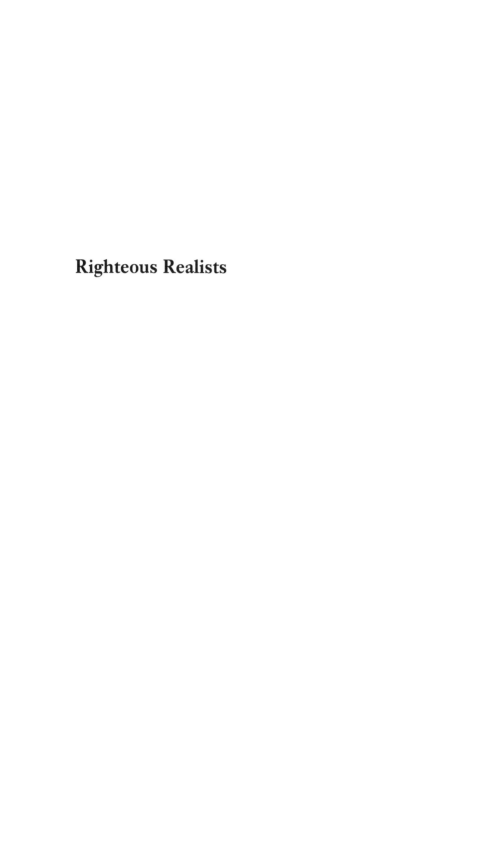

Righteous Realists

Righteous Realists   Political Realis

sponsible Power, and American Culture in the Nuclear Age

Joel H. Rosenthal

Louisiana State University Press

Baton Rouge and London

Designer: Amanda McDonald Key
Typeface: Ehrhardt
Typesetter: Graphic Composition, Inc.
Printer and binder: Thomson-Shore, Inc.

Library of Congress Cataloging-in-Publication Data
Rosenthal, Joel H., 1960–
   Righteous realists : political realism, responsible power, and American culture in the
nuclear age / Joel H. Rosenthal.
      p.   cm. — (Political traditions in foreign policy series)
      Includes bibliographical references and index.
      ISBN 0-8071-1649-1
   1. International relations and culture.   2. International relations—Political aspects.
3. United States—Foreign relations.   4. Realism.   I. Title.   II. Series.
JX1255.R67   1991
327.73—dc20   90-48592
                                                                       CIP

The author is grateful to the University Press of America for permission to reprint
material from his essay "George F. Kennan, the Atom, and the West: Wise Man as
Cultural Critic," which appeared in Kenneth W. Thompson, ed., *Contemporary Politics,
Rhetoric, and Discourse* (Lanham, Md.: University Press of America, 1988).
Quotations from materials in the George F. Kennan Papers, Seeley Mudd Library,
Princeton, N.J., are reprinted by permission of Harriet Wasserman Literary Agency,
Inc., as agents for the author, copyright © 1991 by George F. Kennan.

The paper in this book meets the guidelines for permanence and durability of the
Committee on Production Guidelines for Book Longevity of the Council on Library
Resources. ∞

For my parents

Contents

Foreword

The debate over political realism as an approach to international politics continues. Today's critics propose to modify some aspects of the realist paradigm but appear to accept its main thesis. In the 1950s, critics assailed early realist thinkers as amoral defenders of the European ancien régime. Realism was out of touch with requirements of the new international order. Proponents were antimodern and un-American. Realists were depicted as the cynical destroyers of a new world-wide ethos and of the genius of the American spirit of unity, cooperation, and federalism.

By the 1970s and the 1980s, history had laid waste to most of the substance of this early criticism. The global utopia that realism's opponents had prophesied has not been forthcoming. The international order remains essentially one of recurrent rivalries, alliances, and struggles for power, all commingled with cooperation based on emerging points of convergent interest. As for those who numbered themselves among the early critics of realism, history has passed them by, however popular and appealing their message may have been. Few argue any longer that one brave new world will soon exist or that we live in a new age free of power politics.

One aspect of the postwar criticism, however, deserves continued inquiry and examination. It is the relationship between culture and political thought. The influence of American exceptionalism—the idea that the United States is not like other nations—persists to the present day. It manifests itself in debates over human rights and controversies over intervention anywhere in the world in the name of democracy. According to American exceptionalism, the United States is not like other nations that are subject to the constraints and limits of power. It has both the resources and the responsibility to reach out to others—if not to transform the world, at least to change existing political and economic systems. The United States has the responsibility of helping nations everywhere give birth to new political systems. If democracy is breaking out around the world and free enterprise is replacing communist and socialist regimes, it is because of the Reagan Doctrine and the efforts of official bodies such as the National Endowment for Democracy in the name of these world-wide ends.

What the 1980s have done, then, is to substitute for the idea of a global utopia the concept of a world transformed through a strong American national defense and the propagation of freedom. Leave aside the consequences of a massive and unprecedented federal deficit with its ultimate threat to the economy—a danger of which leaders such as President Eisenhower repeatedly warned—and of foreign-policy and military initiatives in Nicaragua and Panama with costs both material and spiritual that may exceed present calculations. Looking only to the future, the problem is all too apparent. It should be increasingly evident that we have not escaped the imperatives of political realism.

Joel Rosenthal of the Carnegie Council on Ethics and International Affairs and Yale University seeks to probe the relationship between culture and political realism. He brings to his task extraordinary intellectual resources and strengths. He can write. His language is free of encumbering jargon. He is well schooled in historical analysis, his mentor being the distinguished Yale historian Gaddis Smith. Indeed, Yale recognized his earlier work with its award for the university's best doctoral dissertation. As with the majority of authors in the Political Traditions in Foreign Policy Series published by Louisiana State University Press, he stands at the beginning, not the end, of an exciting intellectual journey. Finally, he is searching for interconnections between the social, political, and cultural patterns of the time and the thinkers who wrote about them. His is an inquiry in the grand tradition of humanistic inquiry, not an exercise in linguistic analysis or of correlations in logic. It should be read as one reads enduring traditions and classic works in political philosophy and thought.

Kenneth W. Thompson
Editor, Political Traditions in Foreign Policy Series

Preface

You are not the harsh realist you are painted but the most moral man I know.

—*Walter Lippmann to Hans Morgenthau*

This study originated in questions that grew out of my reading of George Kennan's *The Cloud of Danger* (1977) and *The Nuclear Delusion* (1982). At the time, I wondered how Kennan—a *realist*—could advocate deep reductions in America's nuclear arsenal and urge limited unilateral action by the United States as a first step toward arms control. How could someone so suspicious of the masses endorse a grassroots antinuclear movement and encourage public activism against the arms race? What had happened to Kennan in his later years? What, if anything, had changed? How could the man who coined the term *containment* in 1946 and who frequently expressed his reservations about the efficacy of public involvement in foreign affairs find himself espousing such different ideas late in life?

These questions led inevitably to a questioning of the meaning of realism as it was practiced in post–World War II America. Was realism still a legitimate tradition of political philosophy and consistent with its own classical roots? What could the term *realism* itself mean when the definitive realist, Kennan, went on to take positions such as opposing the Eisenhower-Dulles policies of liberation, rollback, and massive retaliation in the 1950s; denouncing American involvement in Vietnam in the 1960s; and questioning NATO doctrine in the 1970s and early

1980s? After all, these were the litmus-test issues that separated the hard-line realists from the soft, malleable idealists.

A brief inquiry into these matters revealed that Kennan's brand of realism was not about power alone, but about reconciling morality and power. Kennan was among the first to question what "power politics" could possibly mean in a nuclear world, and he found that it could not mean much divorced from moral principles. Indeed, I soon saw that Kennan the realist was also Kennan the steadfast moralist—and that this was the essential point that made his realism both legitimate and coherent. To Kennan, realism did not mean that the strong do what they will and the weak suffer what they must, or that diplomacy must be separated somehow from morality. For him, there could be no separation of the moral from the practical: an amoral conception of realpolitik was unacceptable. Far from draining the moral content from politics, Kennan's realism was all about how to make the moral factors count.

Kennan's career, remarkable for its idiosyncratic twists and turns, was also representative of a trend. He had plenty of company on his quest to transform power politics into a form of "responsible power" commensurate with American values. Hans Morgenthau, Reinhold Niebuhr, and Walter Lippmann all were American postwar realists, and all exhibited tendencies and preoccupations similar to Kennan's and to one another's. All toned down their early cold-war rhetoric as years passed, fighting the excesses of crusading moralism while simultaneously promoting a concept of power politics that retained a moral component at its core. None of the other realists lived as long or traveled as far as Kennan, but many moved in a strikingly similar direction. Although some realists, such as Dean Acheson, emphatically did not change, and others—mostly students of the older realists—turned even more hawkish, a sizable group followed a path that resembled Kennan's, at least in its basic outline. That path and the divergences from it are the subjects of this work.

Surprisingly, neither Kennan nor the other realists changed very much in their basic political philosophy and world view. There was no sudden and paradoxical "turn toward utopia," as some have suggested;

there was no sudden belief in the possibilities of disarmament, democracy, or world government.[1] At the ends of their lives the realists were preaching what they always had preached. Their ethos had remained the same, but like many people in the latter stages of their lives, they felt that the world had changed around them. Kennan's autobiographical summing-up, *Sketches from a Life* (1989), was eloquent testimony to that sense of displacement.

Much of the current work on the modern American realists tends to dwell on the inconsistencies, contradictions, and inadequacies of realism as a political theory. For example, Michael J. Smith's *Realist Thought from Weber to Kissinger* (1986) emphasizes some of the irreconcilable aspects of realism, along with some of the shortcomings that have prevented it from becoming a wholly logical and coherent system. Anders Stephanson takes this tack to an extreme in *Kennan and the Art of Foreign Policy* (1988), using structuralist analysis to deconstruct Kennan's realism into a mass of incongruities. Even Barton Gellman's *Contending with Kennan* (1984), which is based on the premise that Kennan's "claim to consistency should be taken seriously," is devoted to exploring and explaining apparent inconsistencies in Kennan's thought rather than to the philosophical roots of that thought or to Kennan's kinship with other realists.

Like Gellman, I take Kennan's claim to consistency seriously; however, this book represents a searching out of the ties that bind rather than the fragments that deconstruct. Building on a foundation laid by Gellman and others, notably David Mayers in *George Kennan and the Dilemmas of U.S. Foreign Policy* (1989); Richard Fox in *Reinhold Niebuhr: A Biography* (1985); Ronald Steel in *Walter Lippmann and the American Century* (1980); and Kenneth W. Thompson as editor of the sixth edition of Morgenthau's *Politics Among Nations* (1985), I am attempting to present realism as a coherent whole, a way of thinking that has had significant continuity. Among other things, this study illustrates that the evolution of American postwar realism as embodied in

1. See David Gress, "A Turn Toward Utopia," *Commentary,* LXXXIV (July, 1987), 70–72.

the careers of Kennan, Morgenthau, Niebuhr, Lippmann, and others can be explained usefully without becoming entangled in paradox. I do not deny the presence of paradox and even contradiction in realist thought—the realists clearly had a penchant for both—but I do suggest that it may be instructive to start putting realism back together after so many have made so much out of taking it apart.

While highlighting the continuities of realism, this study will neither avoid contradictions nor impose an order that does not emerge on its own. The real story here, however, is not about how the realists changed or how they so often contradicted themselves, but about how they remained the same. The realist Weltanschauung was as constant as could be, and herein, I believe, is the key to understanding postwar American realism. This is not to deny the validity of the narrower theoretical approach, best presented by Michael J. Smith in his brilliantly crafted survey. But it is to suggest—as Smith himself concludes—that realism was more than a theory: it was an expression of a set of beliefs. The tale of how the realists, initially participants in the cold war, became among its most ardent critics is an extraordinary one. What makes it even more extraordinary is that it is not as anomalous as it seems.

Theoreticians become anxious when they detect a conflation between description and prescription; that is, an account of the way something "is" paired with an account of the way it "ought" to be. It is no wonder, then, that the realists have been responsible for a lot of nervous analysts, for the realists had much to say on both scores. Realism did offer a descriptive world view—an account of the way international relations are in fact carried out. With equal potency and often simultaneously, realism also suggested a prescriptive framework for working toward the ideal while living with the real.

To avoid the confusion that the realists themselves engendered, this study proceeds as a deliberately descriptive endeavor: a description of how the realists went about integrating their moral concerns into their practical political judgments, rather than an evaluation of the realists as pure prescriptive theorists. It does not posit realism as a perfectly turned normative theory offering prescriptive solutions or a series of commandments, nor does it seek either to interpret or to judge realism as such a theory. Instead, it describes realism as a product of a particular time and place—a set of values, a web of assumptions, an array of processes of moral reasoning, and a collection of views about America's role in the world.[2]

Because realism sought both to explain and to guide, its integrity and importance might be most clearly revealed on the level of (descriptive) social and cultural analysis. In its historical and cultural context, postwar American realism can be seen as an effort to articulate a set of moral positions and work them out with other, competing claims. The moral positions, or public philosophy, expressed by the realists formed a basis for their thinking about power, ethics, and international affairs, a basis from which they judged policy options. The values and commitments that made up this public philosophy, and the ways in which these were used to forge an idea of the national interest based on responsible power, are the focus of what follows. The particular values espoused by the realists who are mentioned here may or may not be acceptable or relevant today, especially given the changing position of America in the world and the changing mores within American culture itself. Even with the passing of time and the evolution of circumstances, however, the realists' attempt to weave such values into policy surely remains instructive.

2. For a fuller explanation of the virtues of the cultural approach, see Michael Hunt, *Ideology and U.S. Foreign Policy* (New Haven, 1986).

Acknowledgments

This book stands as testimony to the scholarship and example of Kenneth W. Thompson, director of the Miller Center of Public Affairs and Commonwealth Professor of Government at the University of Virginia. For some reason, when an unknown graduate student from out of town appeared at his doorstep unannounced, Professor Thompson took the time to offer some all-important words of encouragement, as well as invaluable practical advice. My gratitude for that welcome and for all that has transpired in the intervening years knows no bounds. I only hope that this book is worthy of his fine example.

I can think of no better mentor than Gaddis Smith, who served as my adviser when, as a graduate student at Yale, I first approached the subject of the postwar realists. He, along with Bruce Russett, devoted considerable time and effort to my work. Their willingness to let me explore the uncharted territory somewhere between history, political theory, and cultural criticism enabled me to take chances that graduate students rarely are afforded.

This book also owes much to those who helped when it was in its most formative stages. Robert Westbrook, probably unbeknownst to him, kept it all together: he introduced me to the possibilities of this kind of study while providing a model of clarity and concision to emulate. I am certain he will take exception to much of what I finally produced, but I hope he still can recognize this study as a product of his teaching.

My colleagues in the American Studies Program at Yale also did much to shape and nurture this project when it needed it most. Marcus

Acknowledgments

Bruce, Glenn Wallach, and James Fisher all gave generously of their time and energies. Each, in his own way, provided the careful mixture of criticism, inspiration, and friendship without which a work like this could never be sustained.

Since moving to the Carnegie Council on Ethics and International Affairs, I also have been fortunate. Robert J. Myers, president of the Council, gave this project his unconditional support from the moment he learned of it. I am grateful for the privilege of working with him and for the opportunities he has made available to me.

I simply would not have been able to complete this work without my right hand at the Council, Matthew Mattern. His research and editing expertise—and his unfailing friendship and good cheer—made working on this manuscript a delight.

Finally, words fail me when it comes to thanking my parents, Edward and Helen Rosenthal, and my wife, Patricia. Their enthusiasm for this book has been extraordinary, and their kindness and generosity made it all possible.

Righteous Realists

1 Political Realism and Its Practitioners
A Political Philosophy for Postwar America

To see through these ideological disguises and to grasp behind them the actual political forces and phenomena becomes, then, one of the most important and most difficult tasks of the student of international politics.
—*Hans Morgenthau, 1948*

It often is considered a compliment, especially in the political world, to be called a realist. The term implies perspicacity and levelheadedness, a commitment to being dispassionate and objective about the issues at hand. To be a realist is to be distinctly this-worldly, to eschew the utopian dreams of impractical idealists. Most politicians and policy makers consider themselves to be realists, for to achieve anything in the political world, even for the most visionary of politicians, it is imperative to face the facts—the *realities*—of any given situation.

Political realism can be more than just the opposite of idealism, however; it can be a philosophy of power and politics in its own right. Throughout history, realist philosophy has had many incarnations, including the variations presented by such luminaries as Thucydides, Machiavelli, Burke, Metternich, and Churchill. The realist heritage is long and venerable, and it should not be surprising that it captured the attention of a group of American thinkers in the late 1940s and early 1950s, when the United States was beginning to come to terms with its new status as a superpower. Along with the nation's new position in the world came the need for an updated American political philosophy capable of dealing with new and complex issues. This need was met in part by those American political realists who created a hybrid political philosophy featuring elements of American pragmatism and European realpolitik. The result was a strand of realism unmistakably American in character, although European in its trappings. The American realists shared more than just an aversion to idealistic proposals and high-minded rhetoric; they also shared a world view.

By itself and without qualification, *political realism* is a virtually useless term. Easily bent or abstracted into meaninglessness, it must be defined with precision if it is to have any value. Perhaps the best example of a well-defined expression of political realism was one of the first that was produced in the postwar era, Hans Morgenthau's *Politics Among Nations* (1948). Morgenthau's treatise, especially as outlined in the opening pages of the second edition (1954), became the classic statement and blueprint of realism, as well as its defining arbiter. These first two editions established Morgenthau as the father of postwar realism in America, and subsequent editions—there have been six editions in all—insured his position as unofficial dean of the realist school.[1]

Morgenthau's thesis was that all human relations, including the relations between states, are based on the struggle for power. "The struggle for power," he wrote, "is universal in time and space and is an undeniable fact of experience."[2] He went on to explain that nations must act in what each determines to be its national interest—and that national interest is best defined in terms of power. After establishing the ubiquity of the struggle for power, Morgenthau suggested that peace could be maintained through two devices: first, the establishment of a stable balance of power; second, an adherence to normative limitations placed on the struggle for power, such as the limitations expressed in international law, codes of international morality, and world public opinion.

In the wake of World War II, however, the German émigré Morgen-

1. Hans Morgenthau, *Politics Among Nations: The Struggle for Power and Peace*, ed. Kenneth W. Thompson (6th ed.; New York, 1985). This most recent edition updates previous volumes by incorporating the work of Morgenthau's later years.

2. Morgenthau, *Politics Among Nations* (1st ed.; New York, 1948), 17.

thau had precious little faith in normative limitations. This is not to say that he abandoned interest in strengthening normative standards; his commitment to such standards remained steady. But the real key to peace, he believed, lay in maintaining a stable balance of power. Normative limitations without a power structure to reinforce them were of little use. Like Hobbes, Morgenthau thought conflict and war were closer to the natural state of man than peace, and he was convinced that the search for peace was a search for equilibrium in the constantly shifting struggle for power among nations. Normative limitations had a role to play in this search and struggle, but only as part of a much larger strategy.

In the first edition, Morgenthau also began to explain his role as a social scientist. The focus of *Politics Among Nations*, he acknowledged, was on the study of social forces, not merely of laws and institutions. "The best the scholar can do," he wrote, "is to trace the tendencies which, as potentialities, are inherent in a certain international situation." Recognizing his role as an analyst and interpreter rather than a purely objective scientist, Morgenthau began to chart the course not only of political realism as a school of thought, but also of the political realist as a member of the academic community. The study of international relations, as Morgenthau saw it, was indeed a social science, but not a science of exact calculations and provable equations. The ambiguous nature of tracing the tendencies of nations made the enterprise more of an art than anything else. In Morgenthau's opinion, the discernment and interpretation of facts was as important to the social scientist as the gathering of the facts themselves.

Morgenthau's view of himself as social scientist and analyst was in keeping with his overarching idea of realism. The political realist, Morgenthau believed, was closely attuned to the irrational impulses present in political life. The realist believed that these impulses periodically raise havoc in an otherwise rational world; further, such upsetting occurrences can be neither regulated nor controlled. The only constant for the realist was, as Morgenthau put it, "the ambiguity of the facts of international politics."[3] If the political idealist assumed that

3. *Ibid.*, 6.

rationality eventually will solve the conflicts arising out of the struggle for power, the realist was more skeptical about the effectiveness of both rationality and the rationalist. For Morgenthau, the challenge was to make sense out of the ambiguities presented by the "facts of international politics." This task would require skill in interpretation and the ability to see beyond the mere facts to the irrational factors present in all political situations.

Political Realism Defined: Morgenthau's Six Principles

The second edition of *Politics Among Nations* was similar to the first but was even more ambitious in its effort to define realism as a theory of international politics. It was also more ambitious—but unfortunately no more clear—in defining the relevance of the normative aspects of the theory. Morgenthau conveniently listed six basic principles of realism in the first chapter, a placement that he retained in later editions of the book. These six principles provided a readily accessible, comprehensive introduction to political realism. A brief summary of them as they were presented in the second edition reveals the essence of Morgenthau's framework:

1. The first principle stated: "Political realism, like society in general, is governed by objective laws that have their roots in human nature." This assertion was as close to positivism as Morgenthau ever got, although it was far from a strictly positivist position. His main point was that theories of politics must be subjected to tests of both reason and experience. There must be a union of theory and practice, for without empirical evidence theory is of little use. This approach called for a rational appraisal of empirical evidence, while it denied the validity of all a priori and abstract theories of behavior. All hypotheses had to be tested against the facts of international politics if a theory of international relations were to be possible.

2. The second principle was perhaps realism's most notorious: "The main signpost that helps political realism to find its way through the landscape of international politics is the concept of na-

tional interest defined in terms of power." In short, power was the preeminent guiding light of foreign policy. This statement was not meant to exclude moral principles as factors in making political decisions, but it made clear which consideration came first. Political realism provided for "a sharp distinction between the desirable and the possible, between what is desirable everywhere and at all times and what is possible under the concrete circumstances of time and place." According to Morgenthau, "Political realism contains not only a theoretical but a normative element. . . . Yet it shares with all social theory the need, for the sake of theoretical understanding, to stress the rational elements that make reality intelligible for theory." By engaging in some deft manipulation, Morgenthau managed to acknowledge the normative element of realism while subordinating it to more immediate power considerations. How Morgenthau managed this and with what consequences is the subject of much of this study.

3. The third principle stated that "realism does not endow its concept of interest defined as power with a meaning that is fixed once and for all." The realist saw the world as fluid, dynamic, and constantly changing. Time and place, as well as culture and context, were vitally important factors in the consideration of any political problem. Morgenthau was emphasizing his belief that realism cannot avoid some measure of contingency: particular exigencies of time and place must receive careful consideration in any analysis of power.

4. According to the fourth principle, "Political realism is aware of the moral significance of political action." Using the reasoning just established in the third principle, Morgenthau now elaborated on what was meant by "moral significance." He unveiled *prudence* as the watchword of realism; indeed, he called prudence the supreme virtue in politics. The fourth principle represented the consequentialist aspect of Morgenthau's approach, stressing the importance of "weighing the consequences of alternative political action." In qualifying the relevance of abstract ethics and doctrinal moral law to the political sphere, Morgenthau suggested that although in ethics one

5

can judge action by its conformity with moral law, in *political* ethics one must judge action in relation to its consequences in the real world. To dramatize his point that the realist must remain aware of the dichotomy between pure ethics and political ethics, Morgenthau cited Abraham Lincoln's oft-quoted statement to the effect that if events proved him wrong, "ten angels swearing I was right would make no difference."

5. The fifth principle proclaimed that "political realism refuses to identify the moral aspirations of a particular nation with the moral laws that govern the universe." This was Morgenthau's warning against the tendencies of nations to be self-righteous about their policies and even messianic in their intentions. His purpose was to argue that realism can cut through the masks of ideology and rhetoric to reveal the underlying motivations of nations. He concluded that "it is exactly the concept of interest defined as power that saves us from that moral excess and that political folly. For if we look at all nations, our own included, as political entities pursuing their respective interests defined in terms of power, we are able to do justice to all of them." By looking at interest in terms of power rather than in terms of moral claims, Morgenthau argued, the realist can gain a better vantage point from which to make political judgments.

6. The sixth principle stated that "the political realist maintains the autonomy of the political sphere, as the economist, the lawyer, the moralist maintain theirs." Economic, legal, and moral concerns were taken into account by the realist, but the first and most important consideration was the political dimension. This was Morgenthau's statement of affirmation: it affirmed the integrity of political science as an independent avenue of inquiry and declared the realist to be a special contributor to political debate. It claimed for the realist his own territory or sphere, wherein political considerations were expected to be supreme. According to Morgenthau, the business of the realist was politics, and all of his analyses must flow from that basic premise. This obligation made for some interesting and unavoidable clashes between spheres.

6

It is clear from a close look at Morgenthau's six principles that political realism concerned more than just power politics. In fact, Morgenthau's list provides an apt illustration of Reinhold Niebuhr's assertion that the realist lives primarily in the "twilight zone" where ethics and politics meet.[4] The obvious tensions—between universality and contingency, between the existence of objective laws and the principle of uncertainty—pointed to the speculative, open-ended quality of realism as Morgenthau conceived it. These tensions and contradictions, far from being debilitating, are instructive. Values questions can be difficult to grasp, and Morgenthau offered a way of ordering them. Along the way, he also made some pointed suggestions as to his preferences in filling in the values variables.

Morgenthau's principles provided a loose framework rather than a rigid doctrine for dealing with this difficult tangle. They offered a way of seeing the world rather than suggesting a definitive interpretation of it.[5] Implicit in these principles were several assumptions about what can be called, for lack of a more precise term, the human condition. In fact, it was these assumptions about man and society that gave the most coherence to his outline of realism and created a strong bond between him and the other realists of his generation.

The Realist World View

The realist world view was dominated by a sense of the tragic. The political realists had few illusions about the possibilities of humanity; they recognized the controlling nature of selfishness and egoism, and believed that such forces were inescapable. Reacting against the Enlightenment faith in the perfectibility of man, the realist held to a quasi-religious image of man as a flawed being aspiring toward perfection but never quite reaching it. Robert McAfee Brown captured the essence of this world view best when he described Reinhold Niebuhr

4. See Reinhold Niebuhr, *Moral Man and Immoral Society: A Study in Ethics and Politics* (New York, 1932).

5. See Kenneth W. Thompson, *Political Realism and the Crisis of World Politics: An American Approach to World Politics* (Princeton, 1960), esp. chap. 1.

as a "pessimistic optimist."[6] Niebuhr and the realists were pessimistic in the sense that they accepted the immediate inadequacies of human beings. They were optimistic because while they accepted the inherent limitations of man, they simultaneously committed themselves to the improvement of the social world in which they as individual human beings lived. Despite their doubts about perfection, they did believe that they could make the world a better place. Not all realists possessed the same degree of optimism that Niebuhr's faith enabled him to sustain, but most were willing to work toward the normative ends that seemed forever to elude them.

Louis Halle, himself a prominent realist, articulated a widely held realist view when he wrote that man is "a beast with a soul, a creature nine parts animal and one part divine whose mission is to overcome the animal element and realize the possibilities of divinity."[7] George Kennan elaborated on this point of view in a 1976 interview: "I have no high opinion of human beings: they are always going to fight and do nasty things to each other. They are always going to be part animal, governed by their emotions and subconscious drives rather than by reason."[8] The animal image was recurrent in realist critiques of human nature; most realists came to see human beings as part beast, held precariously in check by the thin restraint of civilization. The only point of contention among the realists on this subject was the degree to which man could be coaxed out of his bestial tendencies. Some were markedly less sanguine than others about the prospects for such coaxing.

It was also characteristic of realists to be concerned that their theories of human nature and behavior be in agreement with their real-life experiences. Just as Morgenthau sought to justify his theory of international relations by adducing the empirical evidence of history, so too did most realists aim to theorize only from a basis of factual evidence.

6. Robert McAfee Brown, *The Essential Reinhold Niebuhr: Selected Essays and Addresses* (New Haven, 1986).

7. Quoted in Thompson, *Political Realism and the Crisis of World Politics*, 59–60.

8. See George Kennan, *The Nuclear Delusion: Soviet-American Relations in the Atomic Age* (New York, 1982), 72.

The realists preferred that their theories speak to tangible issues and that they personally avoid being sheltered from the world. Dean Acheson put it best in his introduction to Louis Halle's *Civilization and Foreign Policy:* "We are part of something: not something apart. Not gods without but ganglions within. The means and methods we use, the ends we seek, the kind of people we must forever strive to be are all part of the same thing and are inseparable. We are not an end but an intermediary." [9] Acheson gracefully illuminated a fundamental tenet of realism: there is a continuity between theory and practice, and yet it is practice—the striving and the struggle that we experience as "intermediaries"—that is most telling.

Such struggle, the realists reminded us, takes place squarely within the bounds of history. When Acheson said, "We are part of something," the something was civilization in all its grandeur. The realist world view was a historical one, deeply influenced by the patterns and cycles of history. Even when the realists pointed to the possibilities of "becoming"—of achieving one's full potential in this world—such a notion invariably was measured against historical context. The realists remained keenly aware that all human activity takes place within history and is limited inherently by its boundaries. In keeping with the realists' tragic view of man, their tendency to look at the world through the prism of history usually resulted in fixations with the limits of human achievement and the confines of the human environment. The challenge was to work toward an ideal world while at the same time learning to live with human and environmental limitations.

For the realists, man was both "creature and creator"; he was both a product of history and an active agent in the world he inhabits.[10] Although man did maintain *some* autonomy, he could not escape his circumstances. Again, World War II looms as the most logical explanation for this point of view. The war created monumental upheaval

9. See Louis Halle, *The Nature of Power: Civilization and Foreign Policy* (New York, 1955), xxi.

10. For a more complete discussion of man as "creature and creator," see Reinhold Niebuhr, "Faith and the Empirical Method," reprinted in Niebuhr, *Christian Realism and Political Problems* (New York, 1953), 10.

even for those who avoided the worst of its consequences. Stanley Hoffmann, in a fine critique of realist thought, suggested rather persuasively that the realists'—and especially Morgenthau's—interest in history came from a deep desire to understand the forces behind the great trauma of the war.[11]

To read the work of the realists is to read large doses of history. Morgenthau, like other realists, relied heavily on historical example to support his arguments. Drawing most of his evidence from modern European history, he often analyzed the concept of the balance of power by making analogies to the Concert of Europe, and he frequently elucidated the classic dilemmas of statesmanship by referring to problems faced by Churchill. Morgenthau employed American history less often than European, although he was fond of citing the *Federalist* papers and the words of Lincoln. Other realists resorted to history as Morgenthau did, to buttress their points of view, but some, like George Kennan, seemed to study history for its own sake: for its depth, beauty, and pageantry. Kennan's historical scholarship on Soviet-American relations revealed a distinctly realist point of view, but it never became pure polemic.[12] His interest in history appeared to transcend the realists' immediate political agenda, assuming a dimension that was as mystical and literary as it was concrete and practical. The main point, however, is that to read the work of Kennan, Morgenthau, and many other realists is to encounter an outlook that places great importance on the past both in its continuities and its discontinuities with the present.

Surprisingly, it was the discontinuities that provoked the most compelling responses. The realists had a characteristic tendency to dwell on history yet at the same time highlight their alienation from it. They were, as a general rule, antimodernists. They saw the machine age and all it had produced as a potential disaster. Frustrated with the dominance of technology, the flatness of mass culture, and the deterioration

11. Stanley Hoffmann, "An American Social Science: International Relations," *Daedalus*, CVI (Summer, 1977), 41–60.

12. For an example of Kennan's rather aesthetic view of history, see his "History as Literature," *Encounter*, LXVII (April, 1959), 10–16.

of the natural environment, the realists had little faith in scientific progress as a cure for modern social ills. Walter Lippmann devoted an entire book—and, one could argue, his entire life—to constructing a "public philosophy" to counteract what he termed "the acids of modernity."[13] These "acids," according to Lippmann, were the forces that make traditional modes of belief impossible in the modern world, leaving a void in the spiritual life of modern man. Lippmann and the other realists all wanted to believe and have faith; their problem lay in finding something to believe in. Refusing to adhere to either of what they considered to be the blind faiths of nineteenth-century liberalism and twentieth-century rationalism, the realists ventured out on their own. Lippmann's bold attempt at solving the problem of discontinuity did not go unnoticed. The notion of a public philosophy lingered in realist thought throughout the postwar period.

Unhappy with the effects of modern science on culture and yet too sophisticated to dismiss the achievements of the modern age, the realists became cultural critics. They evolved into the consummate "alienated insiders." They were insiders in the sense that they held powerful positions in the mainstream of American society; they were alienated in the sense that they were sharp critics of the mainstream they served. Many of them felt peculiarly outside that mainstream at the very same time that they occupied the traditional corridors of power. George Kennan is perhaps the classic example of this paradox. He has been, to be sure, a "wise man," and Walter Isaacson and Evan Thomas were justified in including him in their book on the so-called wise men.[14] But Kennan has never functioned as an organization man or a traditional man of the Establishment: he has been a sharp critic of American culture and politics for more than forty years, a man who has gone to enormous lengths to register his persistent displeasures. It is precisely this disaffected dimension of his life—his unhappiness with

13. See Walter Lippmann, *A Preface to Morals* (New York, 1929), where Lippmann uses the phrase "acids of modernity" throughout; also see Lippmann, *Essays in the Public Philosophy* (Boston, 1955).

14. Walter Isaacson and Evan Thomas, *The Wise Men: Six Friends and the World They Made: Acheson, Bohlen, Harriman, Kennan, Lovett, McCloy* (New York, 1986).

11

the modern age—that sets him so far apart from other, more typical Establishment figures.

Five Political Realists

A closer look at the lives and work of five key realists, all of whom already have been mentioned, can shed more light on the roots of the realist political philosophy. Hans Morgenthau, Reinhold Niebuhr, Walter Lippmann, George Kennan, and Dean Acheson, as scholars, commentators, and political actors, were formidable and indeed indispensable contributors to the development of realism. Any discussion of realism is enhanced by the inclusion of their individual contributions as well as by accounts of their interaction as a group. To varying degrees, these men knew one another and read one another's work. They were alternately their own most ardent supporters and most incisive critics. They evolved into a group of like-minded men who shared basic assumptions but who sometimes quarreled about particulars. In the long run, their similarities far outweighed their differences, and even their quarrels usually were productive, helping more than hindering the articulation of a realist philosophy of power.

Although realism did become a collaboration of sorts, a case can be made for distinguishing Morgenthau as the group leader. His work established the range and parameters for all those who would follow. Because he was so deliberate in his explanations and so prolific as a scholar and commentator, Morgenthau's name became synonomous with political realism. As pacesetter, clarifier, and sounding board, he wielded great influence. Some observers have suggested that much of the debate in international relations in the 1950s could be characterized as a referendum on Morgenthau's views.[15] Just as the discussion of political realism logically begins with the work of Morgenthau, so too does the discussion of the individual realists; even though Kennan

15. See, for example, Kenneth Thompson's reference to a panel discussion entitled "Morgenthau and His Critics" that took place at the 1955 meeting of the American Political Science Association. Thompson, *Political Realism and the Crisis of World Politics*, 33.

has credited Reinhold Niebuhr with being "the father of us all," Morgenthau had at least equal claim to that title.

In a short piece entitled "Fragment of an Intellectual Autobiography: 1904–1932," Morgenthau wrote of the tumultuous events of his young manhood and of the decisive influences on the formation of his intellect. Quoting at length from an essay written in 1922, when he was a senior in a German gymnasium, Morgenthau told of his experiences as a young man coming of age in post–World War I Germany. "My relationship to the social environment," he wrote, "is determined by three factors: I am a German, I am a Jew, and I have matured in the period following the war."[16] Proud of his German nationality, Morgenthau was, in his early years, fond of his homeland. In many ways he led the life of a typical German student. His father was a veteran of the war, having served on both fronts as a doctor. As in many traditional German families, the father was a dominant, authoritarian figure in the Morgenthau household. The family had felt the ravages of postwar inflation and endured many of the same hardships as their neighbors.[17] From his birth in Coburg in 1904 until his high-school years, Morgenthau's life was much like that of his peers except for one ominous fact: he was a Jew in an increasingly anti-Semitic society.

It is difficult to judge just how prejudice might have affected the young Morgenthau and to what extent it shaped his views, but there can be little doubt that the effect was traumatic and long-lasting. As a sensitive, brilliant, high-school student he was subjected to numerous indignities. While giving the Founder's Day speech at his school—an honor accorded to the student ranking first in the class—Morgenthau was shouted at and spit on, and he was confronted by an aristocrat who held his nose through the entire speech because, as local folklore had it, the Jews had an offensive smell.[18] Such hostility, however, may have

16. Hans Morgenthau, "Fragment of an Intellectual Autobiography: 1904–1932," in Kenneth W. Thompson and Robert J. Myers, eds., *Truth and Tragedy: A Tribute to Hans J. Morgenthau* (New Brunswick, N.J., 1984), 1.
17. For a frank discussion of Morgenthau's early years and his relationship to his parents, see "Bernard Johnson's Interview with Hans J. Morgenthau," *ibid.*, esp. 337–49.
18. *Ibid.*, 347–48.

13

toughened Morgenthau. As he wrote in 1922, "Men who have gotten accustomed to submitting to insults in silence and patiently bear injustices; who have learned to grovel and duck; who have lost their self-respect—such men must have spoiled their character, they must have become hypocritical, false and untrue."[19] He did not want to be such a man. He learned early that to seek truth meant that he was in for a fight. His fondness for the popular phrase that he would later emphasize—"one must speak truth to power"—had early beginnings.

The years following high school were not easy for Morgenthau, but he succeeded in securing for himself a first-rate, broad-based education. After initially studying philosophy at the University of Frankfurt, he went to Munich to pursue a degree in philosophy and law. His first love was literature, but his father forbade him from making it his profession, because it was "too unprofitable." So Morgenthau continued his legal studies and eventually went back to Frankfurt to write his doctoral dissertation, "The International Judicial Function: Its Nature and Its Limits." The dissertation emphasized a theme that Morgenthau would spend the rest of his life elaborating on: the weakness of international law. Significantly, Morgenthau's graduate studies brought him into contact with the work of Max Weber. Weber's influence on Morgenthau was considerable. Weber had, in Morgenthau's words, "all the intellectual qualities I had looked for in vain in the contemporary literature inside and outside the universities."[20]

Trained in the philosophy of law, Morgenthau wound up spending most of his career explaining the discrepancy between legal theory and legal reality. Frustrated by the inadequacies of the legal system and the seemingly arbitrary nature of the courts, he found law to be a sorely insufficient tool in his search for truth. The result was a widening of his field of inquiry until he eventually settled on what is now called the study of international relations. His movement into this field coincided with his immigration to America: after teaching German public law from 1932 to 1935, Morgenthau left Germany, eventually reaching the

19. Morgenthau, "Fragment of an Intellectual Autobiography," *ibid.*, 2.
20. *Ibid.*, 7.

United States in 1937. He taught briefly at Brooklyn College and the University of Kansas before assuming a position as a professor of political science at the University of Chicago. Morgenthau stayed at Chicago for most of his academic life, although he did move to New York late in his career, taking positions at the City University of New York in 1968 and the New School for Social Research in 1974. Morgenthau became a naturalized United States citizen in 1943 and later served as a consultant to the government. From 1949 to 1951, at the request of Kennan (who was the director of the Policy Planning staff until 1950), Morgenthau became a consultant to the State Department. Later, from 1961 to 1965, he served as a consultant to the Defense Department. By the end of his career, his work had taken him well beyond the largely philosophical concerns of his early professional work: he had stepped boldly into the arena of public policy.

Two major works catapulted Morgenthau from obscurity into the limelight. The first was *Scientific Man and Power Politics*, published in 1946. Greeted with mixed reviews and some hostility, it nevertheless established Morgenthau as a powerful voice in political science. The publication of *Politics Among Nations* just three years later solidified his reputation, partly because of the force of his laboriously reasoned argument, partly because of the book's popularity: Soon after its initial publication *Politics* became a widely used textbook, going on to serve as an introduction to international relations for a generation of college students. Throughout the 1950s Morgenthau also published articles frequently in periodicals such as *Commentary*, the *American Political Science Review*, and the *Bulletin of Atomic Scientists*. The Vietnam era brought broader fame to Morgenthau for his fearless expression of his antiwar views. Particularly noted were his criticisms of the Johnson administration's Vietnam policy; these appeared, among other places, in the *New York Times Magazine* and the *New York Review of Books*. He may be best remembered, however, for the debate in which he dueled with McGeorge Bundy, President Johnson's special assistant, in front of a nation-wide television audience.

Morgenthau's rise to prominence did not occur in isolation; he had many friends, allies, and students who influenced him along the way.

One of those exerting the most influence, surely was Reinhold Niebuhr, the man Morgenthau once called "the greatest living political philosopher in America."[21] Like Morgenthau, Niebuhr was of German descent, but Niebuhr was American-born, from a pious Lutheran family devoutly committed to its Christian beliefs. Born in 1892 in the Midwest, he was trained as a theologian at the Yale Divinity School and gained experience as a parish minister in Detroit. Throughout his career he published feverishly and continuously; he also preached and lectured to thousands of congregations and audiences. A man of considerable intellectual range and gifted with a great facility in using both the oral and the written word, Niebuhr excelled as a popular social critic as well as a political philosopher. It seemed that no issue escaped his purview or eluded his grasp. His world view—Christian and universal though it was—was also well suited to deal with secular and particular problems. His vision was monumental: he aimed to combine political realism with the tradition of Christian social ethics. Building on these grand frameworks, Niebuhr commented on some of the most pressing political problems of his time.

In his own "fragment of an intellectual autobiography," Niebuhr wrote that he could not claim to be a theologian, but rather a teacher of Christian social ethics and a defender of Christianity in a secular age.[22] Niebuhr's theology was in fact suspect: it lacked the rigor and discipline of others', including that of his brother H. Richard Niebuhr. Despite this weakness of form, Reinhold Niebuhr succeeded in making Christian theology speak to political realism and the practical problems of modern life. He took it upon himself to show the American public, secular in its ways and beliefs, the resonance of Christian values in the modern age. This message led him to forums such as the journals *Christian Century, Christianity and Society,* and his own *Christianity and Crisis,* as well as to such organizations as Americans for

21. Quoted in Harold Landon, ed., *Reinhold Niebuhr: A Prophetic Voice in Our Time* (Greenwich, Conn., 1962), 109.

22. Reinhold Niebuhr, "Intellectual Autobiography," in Charles Kegley and Robert Bretall, eds., *Reinhold Niebuhr: His Religious, Social, and Political Thought* (New York, 1958), 3.

Democratic Action. The list of organizations in which he participated is long, and the list of publications that printed his work may be even longer. All of his activity was directed toward a single goal: to show that a Christian perspective could contribute to an understanding of the modern world and perhaps help in solving its problems, no matter how unique those problems seemed to be. He called his position "Christian realism."

Niebuhr offered Christian realism as a direct challenge to the liberal idealism that was so pervasive in the United States. Christian realism would not provide a justification for the socioeconomic status quo as liberalism had. In recalling his early professional days, Niebuhr cited his experience as a young pastor close to the struggle of the labor movement in Detroit during the 1920s as having had an eye-opening effect on him. The difficulties of dealing with Henry Ford while also helping the workers adjust to the mechanization of the workplace had shown Niebuhr what he called "the irrelevance of the mild moralistic idealism which [I] had identified with the Christian faith, to the power realities of our modern technical society." Reflecting on his career, Niebuhr wrote, "My early writings were all characterized by a critical attitude toward the liberal world view, whether expressed in secular or Christian terms."[23] It was not until he discovered Augustine, however, that Niebuhr found a way to "emancipate" himself from the overwhelming moral idealism of American Christianity. In the work of Augustine, he found what he needed to develop a Christian perspective on the brutal "power realities" of modern society. Through the unlikely combination of Henry Ford and Augustine, a new strand of Christian realism was born.

What most irked Niebuhr about Ford were his moral pretensions. Ford's five-dollars-a-day wage for laborers gained for him what Niebuhr considered to be a false reputation as a humanitarian.[24] This experience led Niebuhr to be skeptical of moral rhetoric; from that point

23. *Ibid.*, 6–9.
24. For an excellent addition to his intellectual autobiography, see Reinhold Niebuhr, "Some Things I Have Learned," *Saturday Review*, XLVIII (November 6, 1965), 21–22.

on, he made it his business to probe moral arguments in order to explore the power relationships beneath them. In Niebuhr's thinking, liberal optimists had deluded themselves about the realities of ego and power: they were susceptible to being blinded by rhetoric. As a realist, Niebuhr believed it was his duty "to take all factors in a political and social situation which offer resistance to established norms, into account, particularly the factors of self-interest and self-power."[25] As far as he could determine, moral factors meant nothing when divorced from factors such as self-interest. When Niebuhr decided to leave Detroit for an academic career, he carried that point of view with him, and almost all of the arguments he later made concerning domestic and international affairs proceeded from it.

The constant in Niebuhr's political commentary, whether on domestic or international issues, was his Augustinian perspective. Of his magnum opus, *The Nature and Destiny of Man*, Niebuhr wrote, "I was concerned to prove that modern versions of man's nature and fate were at once very different and yet very similar to, interpretations found in classical idealism, and that the Biblical view of man was superior to both classical and modern views."[26] This was a view that first and foremost validated a position of religious faith; it also assumed human depravity. It affirmed that "the human self can only be understood in a dramatic-historical environment," and it emphasized the importance of spiritual continuity with the past. It also affirmed that pure reason and rationalization are inherently limited as means to achieving true, transcendent selfhood. Parting company with the classical philosophers, Augustine had concluded that pure reason cannot explain all that needs to be explained. Augustine's battle against the excessive rationalism of the classical philosophers mirrored Niebuhr's own battle against the excessive rationalism of both Marxism and Deweyan liberalism. Augustinian realism proposed the recognition of the benefits of reason, but not the worship of reason; worship was reserved for

25. Reinhold Niebuhr, "Augustine's Political Realism," reprinted in Niebuhr, *Christian Realism and Political Problems*, 119.

26. Niebuhr, "Intellectual Autobiography," in Kegley and Bretall, eds., *Reinhold Niebuhr*, 9.

God. To Niebuhr, who was fighting against the deification of scientific analyses in modern culture, Augustine provided an attractive, usable model.

The paradoxes Niebuhr so brilliantly illuminated in his writing were an integral part of his own life.[27] Niebuhr moved dialectically between theory and practice, reason and faith, optimism and pessimism. He never settled on an absolute, except when it came to final faith in God. Ironically, in spite of his message of faith and humility, he achieved great fame. (At the height of his celebrity he was featured on the cover of *Time* magazine.) With his reputation established, he became much sought after as a lecturer, particularly on college campuses. He also was pursued by politicians such as John Kennedy, who, when looking for Protestant support in his bid for the presidency, turned to Niebuhr for approval. Partisan politics and his image as a celebrity aside, Niebuhr probably will be best remembered for his books. *Moral Man and Immoral Society, The Nature and Destiny of Man, The Children of Light and the Children of Darkness,* and *The Irony of American History* are paradoxical in themselves. Although they are period pieces, reflective of the times in which they were produced, they also shed light on the timeless quality of the human condition.

Even more popular than Reinhold Niebuhr was the well-known newspaper columnist Walter Lippmann. A fixture on the American political scene for more than fifty years, Lippmann became a household name primarily through his syndicated newspaper column, "Today and Tomorrow." His career in journalism was complemented by his publication of a number of books and weighty academic pieces that solidified his reputation as political commentator and distinguished him from other daily newspaper journalists. As he matured, Lippmann became widely accepted by the American public and by many political leaders around the world as an authority on American politics. Born in 1889 and greatly influenced by the events of World War I, Lippmann made one of his great achievements in helping to develop a vision of realpolitik for the United States in world affairs.

27. For a complete account of the importance of paradox in Niebuhr's life and work, see Richard W. Fox, *Reinhold Niebuhr: A Biography* (New York, 1985).

19

Lippmann was never able to sustain a faith like Niebuhr's, but he did manage to temper his brand of realism with a concept of "a higher law." In his "public philosophy," secular though it was, he recognized the need to transcend the purely immediate and practical concerns of everyday life. A nonpracticing, assimilated Jew, Lippmann struggled for most of his life to find something in the spiritual realm in which to believe. From *Preface to Politics* (1913) to *Essays in the Public Philosophy* (1955), he devoted a great deal of energy to matters of faith and belief in the modern world.

Lippmann's career was illustrious from the start. As a brilliant Harvard undergraduate he caught the eye of the fabled William James. Before leaving Harvard in 1910, he developed relationships with George Santayana and the eminent British thinker Graham Wallas. Lippmann moved easily in such company, thriving on the intellectual stimulation. Soon after graduation he took a job working for another man of considerable stature, the muckraking journalist Lincoln Steffens. Lippmann's career got its most important boost when he was asked by Herbert Croly to join the staff of the fledgling *New Republic* magazine in 1914. For the next fifty years, at the *New Republic* and numerous other publications, he would remain in the public eye commenting on public affairs. He relished having free rein to comment as he pleased, beholden to no one except his reading public. As a part of the political establishment yet entirely independent of it, Lippmann became one of the founders of a new breed of journalists. He was one of the original twentieth-century political pundits of the mass media. He has inspired many imitators since, but few if any equals.[28]

Lippmann's contribution to political realism was far-reaching. Because of the length of his career and the fact that he was so prolific, a study of the evolution of Lippmann's views could provide a reasonably complete picture of the development of realism. His views on human nature, democracy, and the mass media, among many other topics, are well documented and similar to those of other realists discussed in this

28. For an account of Lippmann's background and career, see Ronald Steel, *Walter Lippmann and the American Century* (Boston, 1980).

20

work. One concept, however, stands out in Lippmann's critique of foreign affairs, and it has come to be associated with his name: realpolitik. In three of his major books on United States foreign policy, *The Stakes of Diplomacy* (1915), *U.S. Foreign Policy: Shield of the Republic* (1943), and *U.S. War Aims* (1944), Lippmann argued for an American foreign policy based on this idea usually associated with Continental statesmen.

It is significant that Lippmann's first book on American foreign policy, *The Stakes of Diplomacy,* began with an epigraph taken from Admiral Alfred T. Mahan. By invoking Mahan on the large issue of "temptation and impulse to war," Lippmann was tipping his hand immediately: he would be speaking the language of geopolitics. Mahan was an American naval officer turned historian who saw the world in geopolitical terms and had gained prominence by arguing for strong military protection for America's vital interests. He was a forceful advocate of the idea of insuring national well-being through strength, and he believed that the United States had to use its power to protect its interests. Interests, Mahan concluded, were more often than not determined by geopolitical realities. Lippmann was clearly in the Mahan tradition. His book addressed the problem of stability in international relations, in particular the problem of the destabilizing effects of the newly created political vacuums in the raw-material-rich third world. Like Mahan, Lippmann saw international relations as a struggle for survival between nations. Also like the admiral, Lippmann believed that war could be avoided only by delicately balancing the power and interests of competing nations.

Stability was the key for Lippmann; to create a stable system—a structure—was his goal. Such a system, he hoped, would diffuse the intensity of the struggle between nations and reduce the chances for conflict. "Peace," he believed, "is to be had as a result of wise organization." This, of course, was written before America's involvement in World War I and before Lippmann's own involvement in the American effort to secure a peace after the war. In 1915, Lippmann still had faith in the possibilities of a formalized international organization—faith he would lose later when the League of Nations disappointed him. Yet despite the shortcomings of the League as a mechanism for facilitating peaceful coexistence, Lippmann never gave up his basic belief that peace was based on *structure*, whether through a formal organization such as the League (which was unlikely to succeed) or through an informally enforced balance of power (which was more likely to do so). As he wrote in his chapter titled "A Little *Realpolitik*," the "supreme task of world politics is not the prevention of war, but a satisfactory organization of mankind. Peace will follow from that. That is, in fact, what peace is."[29]

Realpolitik, as Lippmann went on to explain it, involved more than organization and balancing power between states; it also involved recognizing self-interest and then protecting it. He made this idea explicit in *U.S. Foreign Policy*, written at the height of World War II. Lippmann was concerned not only with balancing power between the United States and its foes, but also with balancing America's own power with its commitments. "We must be sure," he wrote, "that we know what we mean by a foreign commitment and by the power to balance it." Lippmann sounded a warning to Americans that American interests had grown and that as a nation the United States had to be willing to support its new interests and commitments with its power. A return to isolation after the war would not do. "The thesis of this book," wrote Lippmann, "is that a foreign policy consists in bringing into balance, with a comfortable surplus of power in reserve, the nation's commitments and the nation's power."[30] This would become, in time, a classic definition of foreign policy and would serve as a starting point for postwar thinkers speculating on modern interpretations of "the national interest."[31]

During and after World War II, Lippmann continued to stress concepts he had introduced thirty years earlier in *The Stakes of Diplomacy:* structure, order, systems, balance. Increasingly skeptical about the

29. Walter Lippmann, *The Stakes of Diplomacy* (New York, 1915), 211, 224.
30. Walter Lippmann, *U.S. Foreign Policy: Shield of the Republic* (Boston, 1943), 9.
31. See, for example, Paul Kennedy, *The Rise and Fall of the Great Powers: Economic Change and Military Power from 1500 to 2000* (New York, 1987), and Samuel Huntington, "Coping with the Lippmann Gap," *Foreign Affairs*, LXVI (Winter, 1987–88), 453–77.

possibilities for formal international cooperation, he clung to his real-politik alternative. In *U.S. War Aims*, essentially a continuation of *U.S. Foreign Policy*, Lippmann asserted that effective international organization in the postwar world meant a recognition of spheres of influence. He believed that the establishment of spheres of influence would reduce tensions between nations since each of the great powers would then have its own domain, clearly delineated as such. Each power would have spheres only as large as it viably could protect and control. Lippmann was greeted with much opposition at the time, but his vision coincided with what eventually evolved in the postwar world. Geopolitician that he was, his suggestion of spheres of influence was consistent with his view of international relations, a view reaching as far back as his first publications on the subject. Admiral Mahan would have found much to admire in Lippmann's wartime and postwar views.

After the war, Lippmann further refined his views with the publication of *The Cold War* (1947), a slender volume comprising a series of columns he had written in response to George Kennan's "X" article, "The Sources of Soviet Conduct." Lippmann argued for the careful calibration of military and political commitments. He warned that meeting every Soviet threat all over the globe with "unalterable counterforce" was a recipe for overextension and disaster. Lippmann called for American policy makers to choose their areas of commitment and not to spread American resources too thin around the globe.

It was ironic that Lippmann's trenchant criticism turned out to be directed at the work of Kennan. The two men's disagreement over early versions of containment was more technical than substantive. In fact, Kennan agreed with much of Lippmann's critique. While Lippmann was writing his columns, Kennan, as head of the State Department's Policy Planning staff, was preparing policy that was closer to Lippmann's *The Cold War* than to his own "X" article.[32] Lippmann was more careful, analytical, and precise than Kennan in articulating his notion of containment. He could afford to be. Kennan, it must be

---

32. See John Lewis Gaddis, *Strategies of Containment: A Critical Appraisal of Postwar American National Security Policy* (New York, 1982).

remembered, wrote the "X" article largely out of the text of his "Long Telegram" of 1946, a document produced principally for the purpose of persuasion. From his vantage point in the United States embassy in Moscow, Kennan saw an urgent need to jolt the policy makers in Washington out of what he saw as their unwarranted optimism concerning Soviet intentions for the postwar world.

Kennan, like Lippmann and Niebuhr, attained a stature rarely achieved in American culture. Like both Lippmann and Niebuhr, he was blessed with longevity and a prolific pen, both of which helped him establish a reputation as a "wise man." Today, Kennan is universally respected for his knowledge of Russian history and Soviet-American relations. Although many critics have disagreed strongly with him through the years, he still is acknowledged widely as an elder statesman and sage. Born in 1904 in Wisconsin, Kennan graduated from Princeton in 1925 and then joined the newly restructured Foreign Service. After basic training as an officer in that service, he became a Russian specialist, receiving special training in Russian language, literature, and history. Kennan's State Department postings in the 1930s and 1940s brought him to a variety of cities in Eastern Europe, including Moscow in 1934. It was his second tour of duty in Moscow, beginning in 1944, that eventually put him in the spotlight: during that second tour he wrote the Long Telegram featuring, among other things, the concept of containment.

Kennan's career has been a distinguished one, highlighted by his positions as director of the first Policy Planning staff under secretaries of state George Marshall and Dean Acheson (1947–1950); as ambassador to the Soviet Union (1951–1952); and as a professor at the Institute for Advanced Study at Princeton University. His professional life has been punctuated by the publication of numerous books, among them *American Diplomacy, 1900–1950* (1951), which has become a classic in American diplomatic history. In effect, Kennan has pursued three careers: those of government official, political commentator, and historian. His last stint in government service, his ambassadorship to Yugoslavia, ended in 1963. Since then he has devoted himself to the study of Russian history, Soviet-American relations, and current political problems. Along the way he has received numerous awards, including the Pulitzer Prize and the National Book Award, and many honorary degrees.

Yet Kennan's path to fame has been filled with unexpected turns. For example, he is best known as the author of containment, but his version of this concept is quite different from the versions of those who have sought to invoke containment as orthodox military doctrine. In fact, in recent years, Kennan has retreated to a quasi-isolationist position. He has spent most of his life warning of the "evils of utopian enthusiasms," only to be accused himself of wishful thinking, especially on issues concerning nuclear weapons.[33] Despite their being frequently misunderstood and dismissed, Kennan's views always have attracted attention. His uncommon lucidity, combined with his willingness to tackle the most difficult problems in American foreign policy, is part of what distinguishes him from others. The other part is his absolute willingness to take unpopular positions. All of this has made Kennan a major participant in many of the fiercest political debates of his time. Raising troublesome problems and proposing controversial solutions can be exasperating, and Kennan has experienced his share of frustration. His critics have been severe with him, particularly on his alleged inconsistencies. There may be some truth to these critics' claims, but it does seem clear that there has been an overall coherence to his world view.[34] He has shared, with Morgenthau and others, a realist conception of human nature and politics, as well as a consistent hierarchy of values, and his positions on particular issues have arisen essentially from those basic views.

Among Kennan's most important contributions to political realism are his suggestions on how policy makers should approach their task. It was Kennan who wrote that "we must be gardeners and not mechanics in our approach to world affairs. We must come to think of the

33. For Kennan's views on "the evils of utopian enthusiasms," see George Kennan, *Realities of American Foreign Policy* (Princeton, N.J., 1954), esp. 21–22.
34. For a discussion of inconsistency and coherence in Kennan's world view, see Barton Gellman, *Contending with Kennan: Toward a Philosophy of American Power* (New York, 1984).

development of international life as an organic and not a mechanical process."[35] The organic metaphor was especially appropriate for the realists, who believed in the use of reason but also recognized the influence of other aspects of human nature, such as irrationality and egoism. Kennan feared social engineering, which he thought took too little account of the quirks and unpredictability of human existence. Kennan preferred policy makers who were flexible in their thinking to social engineers who built rigid mechanisms. Success would be achieved by cultivating one's own garden—by working with the forces of nature instead of trying to dominate them.

Another of Kennan's many contributions to political realism is his refinement of the concept of the national interest. Much of Kennan's writing has been devoted to exposing how American national interest has been distorted by politicians seeking political gain. According to Kennan—and most of his realist colleagues would concur—American policy makers more often than not have hidden themselves under the mask of ideology. They have clothed their policies in politically attractive terms, selling those policies as moral imperatives to a public that responds to such emotional appeals for justice. The true national interest often has been lost in the rhetoric, perhaps intentionally. In *American Diplomacy,* Kennan dissected this problem in detail. From the Open Door policy (justified by its supporters in terms of protecting China's territorial rights) to the American policy of unconditional surrender that was needed to assuage the public's moral outrage that led to the nation's entry into both world wars, Kennan demonstrated America's utter need to justify its actions on moral and legal terms.

Kennan has had no complaint with moral and legal justifications of behavior so long as they have been sincere and narrowly defined; people *should* act morally and legally. What he has found fault with is the use of such justifications as screens for power considerations. He has been equally wary of utopians who believe that a moralistic-legalistic approach to international affairs actually can be an effective one—that nations can be induced to act solely on principle rather than

35. Kennan, *Realities,* 93.

self-interest. Such a conception of international relations is contrary to all of Kennan's thinking. So whether moralistic-legalistic arguments are used as masks or as legitimate bases for policy, Kennan has doubted their effectiveness.

In essence, Kennan has defined his brand of realism by pitting it against a moralistic-legalistic world view. Unfortunately, this has led to some confusion about his views on morality and foreign policy.[36] Himself a highly principled and moral man, Kennan has been anything but amoral in his attitudes about private life and public policy. What he *has* opposed is the misuse of morality as a concept and a principle. He has seen too many crusades and causes and too many self-righteous politicians to be taken in by utopian rhetoric. Moralism, Kennan has argued, too often has been used merely to mobilize the public; it has obfuscated more often than it has clarified.

Superficially at least, Kennan would seem to have had an alter ego on this problem in Dean Acheson, the secretary of state whom Kennan once advised from his policy-planning post in the State Department. In theory, Acheson agreed with Kennan that "the language of moral discourse—colored as it is apt to be at one end with fervor and at the other with self-righteousness—is more likely to obscure than clarify our discussion."[37] Like Kennan, Acheson saw that the "delusive simplicity" of many moral arguments could lead to dangerous conclusions.[38] Specifically, he was concerned about politicians who were using moral arguments against postwar military commitments in Europe as well as against the development of nuclear weapons. As a realist, Acheson preferred a Lincolnesque approach: one that would take moral considerations into account but would not subordinate all else to them. Although in theory Acheson and Kennan agreed, in practice they did not. Acheson was more willing than other realists to fight fire

36. For Kennan's latest clarification of this issue, see George Kennan, "Morality and Foreign Policy," *Foreign Affairs*, LXIV (Winter, 1985–86), 205–19.

37. Dean Acheson, *Power and Diplomacy* (Cambridge, Mass., 1958), 108.

38. For more on Acheson's views on the danger of excessive moralism in foreign policy see Dean Acheson, "Morality, Moralism, and Diplomacy," *Yale Review*, XLVII (Summer, 1958), 481–93.

with fire. If opportunists would argue in moral terms, he would match them. As a principal in the development of the Truman Doctrine and NSC-68 (the Truman administration's blueprint for national defense), Acheson used plenty of moral rhetoric in marketing his product.

Acheson's marketing techniques found no favor with Kennan, who objected, for example, to the universality in both the wording and intent of the Truman Doctrine. Kennan disapproved of the sweeping rhetoric of the doctrine, which suggested that in the postwar world nations would be forced to "choose between alternative forms of life" and that the choice would be a stark one: freedom or subjugation. Kennan was skeptical about the statement that the United States "must assist free peoples to work out their own destinies in their own way." [39] Kennan found this language (and the argument it implied) unacceptable; it was too broad and undiscriminating. He would have preferred a narrower doctrine that stated limited and concise objectives. In 1947, however, it was apparent that limited language would not get the job done. A broader conceptualization of the problem and an all-inclusive method of argumentation would be necessary to achieve the administration's immediate political goal of securing aid for Communist-threatened Greece and Turkey.

In 1947, congressional and public opinion did not favor extending America's overseas commitments. If the United States was to play a role in global affairs, a rallying point was needed. With the Truman Doctrine and its provision for assistance to Greece, Turkey, and other threatened nations, the Truman administration provided such a rallying point. Using an early version of the domino theory, Acheson rescued the foreign-aid plan in a now-famous meeting between administration officials and congressional leaders. At first the plan was in trouble: the congressional delegation could not be convinced to support it. But with the plan going down to defeat, Acheson—at the time

39. For a more complete version of Kennan's reaction to the Truman Doctrine, see George Kennan, *Memoirs, 1925–1950* (Boston, 1967), 314–21, Vol. I of Kennan, *Memoirs*, 2 vols. For more on the immediate context of the Truman Doctrine, see Richard M. Freeland, *The Truman Doctrine: Foreign Policy, Domestic Politics, and Internal Security, 1946–1948* (New York, 1971), esp. chap. 2.

the undersecretary of state—took the floor and made an impassioned plea. If Soviet pressure succeeded in the region, he said, "like apples in a barrel infected by the rotten one, the corruption of Greece would infect Iran and all the East." Acheson had struck the right chord. Senator Arthur Vandenberg, a key member of the delegation, responded: "If you say that to the Congress and the country, I will support you and I believe that most of its members will do the same." [40] By resorting to a universal argument couched in moral terms, Acheson succeeded in convincing Congress and the American people of the need for foreign aid.

Kennan and Acheson would disagree on more than just the rhetoric of the Truman Doctrine and the rationales given for American policy in the late 1940s. The two men later had titanic struggles over the fate of Germany, the development of the H-bomb, and the recognition of Communist China. Yet somehow, after their struggles were decided one way or the other, their mutual respect remained intact. This amity may have followed from the fact that despite their disagreements, they held the same fundamental world view. The difference between them had more to do with practical political strategies than with basic beliefs. Acheson, the more politically astute of the two, was an expert practical operator, willing and able to read the political climate and sell his policies accordingly. Kennan, less politically nimble, frequently found himself on the outside looking in.

Acheson's background was similar to Kennan's, although Acheson never experienced discomfort or alienation as he made his way through the traditional corridors of power. Born in 1893, Acheson graduated from three of America's finest schools: Groton, Yale, and Harvard Law School. The son of an Episcopal minister, Acheson was not born to wealth or privilege, but he was exposed to both circumstances early in life, and he learned to move comfortably in elevated circles. At Harvard, Acheson became acquainted with Felix Frankfurter, who recommended him for a job as a clerk for Supreme Court justice Louis Bran-

40. For more on Acheson's role in the early stages of the Truman Doctrine, see Dean Acheson, *Present at the Creation: My Years in the State Department* (New York, 1969), 217–19.

deis. After two years with Brandeis and a stint as a private lawyer, Acheson entered government service in 1933 as undersecretary of the treasury. In 1941 he became an assistant secretary of state, working on lend-lease agreements and the Bretton Woods Conference among other things, and in 1945 he was made undersecretary of state. With the election of Truman in 1948, Acheson was appointed secretary of state; he remained in that office until the end of Truman's term. Acheson then returned to private life, but like Morgenthau, Niebuhr, Lippmann, and Kennan, he also became an active elder statesman. Widely respected for his knowledge and experience, he often was called upon to give advice on foreign-policy matters. On at least two occasions Acheson found himself back in the middle of major policy decisions. During the Cuban missile crisis President Kennedy enlisted his services, and President Johnson sought his counsel at various times during the Vietnam War.[41]

Acheson's view of foreign policy was greatly influenced by the tradition of men like Henry Stimson who served before him. Ever the gentleman public servant, Acheson carried with him a sense of noblesse oblige. Like Stimson, he believed in the virtues of decent and civilized behavior, and he loathed duplicity of any kind. Acheson held that, ideally, the conduct of nations should not have to be much different from the conduct of gentlemen. "We must act straightforwardly, candidly, and honestly," he wrote. Quoting the English statesman Lord Cecil, Acheson continued, "Perhaps what we do is less important than how we do it." The emphasis was on means rather than ends. "The ends of action are not, for the most part, determined by ideals," he concluded, "but the other way around."[42] One can imagine Acheson nodding approvingly at Stimson's apocryphal statement that "gentlemen do not read each other's mail." To be a gentleman meant to uphold certain standards of behavior, to act in a certain way. From proper form, all else would follow.

41. For more biographical information on Acheson, see Gaddis Smith, *Dean Acheson*, (New York, 1972); Ronald Steel, "Acheson at the Creation," *Esquire*, C (December, 1983), 206–215; and Isaacson and Thomas, *Wise Men*.

42. Acheson, "Morality, Moralism, and Diplomacy," 493.

Acheson's political realism was exhibited in his statements against moral crusading and the need to favor means over ends, but it was most evident in his accomplishments, and nowhere more clearly so than in his attention to the problem of the balance of power. Perhaps because of his training as a lawyer, Acheson preferred to concentrate on individual cases rather than to deal with abstract theories, and while in office he focused on the problems presented by the Truman Doctrine, the Marshall Plan, the Korean War, the Communists in China, and the NATO alliance, among other things. Nearly all of these problems were considered as pieces of a larger problem: maintaining the balance of power in the ever-changing postwar world.

Acheson's *Power and Diplomacy* (1958), when considered along with his diplomatic achievements, showed him to be a classic realist. In the book, Acheson argued for a fluid foreign policy, one that would be capable of change as the world changed around it. Like his realist colleagues, he invoked the Concert of Europe as a useful analogy for his times. In warning against lapses in vigilance toward Communist aggression, he introduced such concepts as "counterpower." Acheson argued for a policy that would insure "a workable system of free states" that could keep markets open and resist Communist control. As he saw it, the United States had a choice: Americans could "use their vast productive power, along with their own hard work, to maintain their preeminence and to fashion a system by which they and all who have the will to do so [can] be strong and free," or they could "expend their productive power on an increase in consumption and leisure, leaving the non-Communist world leaderless, to drift along as best it can."[43] Given the phrasing of the alternatives, it was clear which path Acheson preferred.

Acheson's realism was based on his firm belief that America simply could not afford to return to isolationist ways in the postwar world. The United States had to recognize its position as the preeminent industrial and military power in the world and act accordingly to protect its interests. What Acheson feared most was that the nation might not be will-

43. Acheson, *Power and Diplomacy*, 23.

ing to make the sacrifices it needed to make as the leader of the free world. Throughout his career in government, he did everything in his power to insure that such a failure of will would not happen. As a realist, he was most skeptical of what appeared to be quick fixes and simple solutions. He opposed various arms-control agreements when he found them disadvantageous to the United States, and he looked upon institutions such as the United Nations as instruments of negotiations and nothing more. In Acheson's view, the United States could not, through the force of its own will, reduce the nuclear threat or raise the UN to a stature that it did not have. Arms control required cooperation between nations, as did an effective UN. Prudence, in every situation, was the best policy; wishful thinking was not. For Acheson, one of the greatest threats to the United States was the false prophet—the crusader who based his belief on simple moral arguments.

Righteous Realists

The political realists recognized and preached that all people live in a world of competing moral claims. The realists articulated this idea perhaps better than any of their contemporaries, and they put forward hundreds of concrete proposals for ways in which individuals and nations could live in such a world. As Niebuhrians schooled in the ways of the "children of darkness," they realized that political action was fraught with evil consequences. To act morally, they concluded, was often to choose the lesser of two evils. They believed that in the postwar world it was the "children of light" who should be feared: those who were blinded by optimism, sentimentality, and facile reasoning, those who thought they had "truth." On the Left, these people included pacifists, scientific rationalists, Wilsonian liberals, and One Worlders; on the Right, McCarthyites, isolationists, and supernationalists. All were thought to be equally dangerous. The realists' world view was not as clear-cut as that of their opponents: the realists saw shades of gray where those opponents saw only black and white.

The realists made their reputation exposing false gods and the false prophets who promoted those gods. They criticized the crusading nature of American foreign policy as it was expressed on both ends of the political spectrum, and they warned against naïveté. Ironically, the realists criticized American foreign policy for being too American—too puritanical, too crusading, and too sure of American exceptionalism. They questioned both the missionary zeal of American policy makers and the presumption that foreign affairs could be governed by American standards of political morality. The realists saw a United States that was playing a world-wide game by its own rules, ignorant of the fact that its opponents might follow another rulebook entirely. What the United States needed was a lesson in power politics. Not surprisingly, the realists looked to European models.

It is significant that the realists included Morgenthau, a German-Jewish émigré; Niebuhr, a second-generation German-American Lutheran; Lippmann, an assimilated American Jew of German descent; and Kennan, a somewhat alienated American intellectual who spent a great deal of his adult life overseas. Thus, all of the realists mentioned in this chapter, with the possible exception of Acheson, had an outsider's perspective. Although they rose to prominence within the Establishment, their experience had an added dimension: They all had a personal awareness of American exceptionalism; they knew what it was like to be a part of another culture and to struggle with adapting to mainstream American life. They could see more clearly than most the Puritan strain and the moral rhetoric, and they could see how it shaped the American perspective on international relations.

To their credit, the realists sought to remedy the situation by preaching humility. Niebuhr was especially outspoken in this regard. He wrote often about the dangers of the "pride and self-righteousness of power nations," calling these nations' prideful tendencies "a greater hazard to their success in government than the machinations of their foes."[44] The solution, according to Niebuhr, lay in recognizing a power greater than oneself. For the Christian, that power was God; for the nation, it was the forces of international relations, over which any one

44. Reinhold Niebuhr, "The Illusion of World Government," reprinted in Niebuhr, *Christian Realism and Political Problems*, 30.

nation could have only limited control. The United States could not be the final arbiter of international conflict any more than an individual Christian could be the final judge of the morality of his actions. The ultimate word must be left to a higher authority, be it God, history, or some other entity. The important point was that nations, like individuals, can have only partial knowledge and must make decisions based on what they know at a given time. With this in mind, they should never claim that their decisions are universally applicable. They should state their values, put them forth with confidence and conviction, and act in accordance with them—but always with a measure of humility.

It is ironic that the realists, who warned against self-righteousness, obsessive moralizing, and false prophets, became prophets themselves. Their message was delivered as a jeremiad, not unlike that of the Puritans. Like its Puritan predecessor, the realist jeremiad was a political sermon filled with social criticism. The realists' criticism, however, ultimately affirmed the American experiment rather than refuting it. Far from being all gloom and despair, it served as both a justification of the American experiment and a unifying cultural force.[45] The realists criticized American foreign policy for its presumption of American exceptionalism, but in the process they became quintessential American exceptionalists themselves.

As exceptionalists, the realists—like John Winthrop before them—saw America as "a city on a hill," with the eyes of all the world upon it. As Winthrop had envisioned it in 1630, America was to be a shining example of community, a model for the rest of the world to follow. Americans were to be God's new chosen people, fulfilling a new mission in a new world. That mission was to live morally and righteously, and to show the old and corrupt nations of the world that God's work could indeed be done on earth.

Although less fundamentalist in their views and less prone to draw direct biblical analogy than the Puritans, the realists did believe in the specialness of America. They believed that America was capable of

45. For more on the American jeremiad, see Sacvan Bercovitch, *The American Jeremiad* (Madison, Wis., 1978).

sustaining the highest standards of political morality, and they thought that America still could be the role model other nations could follow. Nevertheless, for the realists exceptionalism was most useful as an internal model for community living; it did not translate directly into a belief that America was endowed with a special moral role in world affairs. To a large extent, in fact, the belief in exceptionalism had to be restrained when it came to world affairs. The realists knew that to treat the United States as a special actor in world affairs was dangerous. Morality, they knew, was a relative thing: every nation believes it is morally justified when it acts. Better to stay with America as an example, an illustration of an ideal. To lead by example was infinitely better than to expect all nations to believe that the United States had a special moral standing in world affairs.

The realists set about constructing a view of the world in which the United States would be an important political actor but not one fixated on imposing its own internal standards on the rest of the planet. Their task was to create a foreign-policy structure that reflected American morality without allowing a sense of moral superiority to dominate the endeavor. Morality was a factor in their recommendations, of course, as was their faith in America as a unique and virtuous country. But they never let faith in American morality change their views about the way world affairs are conducted. The United States, they maintained, was like any other nation: its claims of exceptionalism were lost in a sea of other nations proclaiming the same thing. The key was to have a foreign policy that embodied American values without forcing those values on others.

Never especially self-righteous, the realists were righteous nonetheless. Their world view included the concept of competing moral claims, but it was not without a hierarchical structure. After the realists developed their ideas about how morality should affect foreign policy, they defended those ideas with vigor. *Righteous realists* is not meant to be a derogatory appellation for these men. It merely indicates the moral component implicit in their realism. All of the five realists on whom this work focuses were attuned to moral issues in their personal lives and made morality a central theme in their writings on world affairs. In choosing morality as a key concept and the jeremiad as their medium, they were working within a distinctly American tradition. And whether they were aware of it or not, they were promulgating a new strain of American exceptionalism.

The best way to illustrate this point—and to see through the realists' own ideological disguises—is to look at the realists in action as they incorporated moral considerations with their theory of power politics. Indeed, part of the purpose of this study is to search beyond this "power politics" label to determine just what the realists meant when they used the term. It is my contention that they wanted to make power politics both palatable to American tastes and consistent with the highest of American ideals—to turn power politics into *responsible* power politics. As I see it, the realists' main contribution to American political thought was their development of the concept that I will call the *responsible use of power.*

2 Responsible Power

I am afraid that when I think about foreign policy, I do not think in terms
of doctrines. I think in terms of principles.
—*George Kennan, 1967*

In one respect, the realists' choice of power as their primary focus was
a curious one, given their abhorrence of abstractions. "Power" and
"power politics" can be thought of as purely theoretical constructs, annoyingly general in their connotations. One critic, the political scientist
Charles McClelland, went so far as to say that "with rare exceptions,
the users of power explanations of international politics have only a
misty notion of what they are talking about. Power is an arousing and
poetic symbol capable of evoking a wide range of feelings, fears, satis-
factions and discontents in people without contributing, however, to
any genuine understanding." [1] McClelland had a point, although he
probably overstated it. At times the realists did succumb to abstraction,
and they did engage in some crusading while hiding behind the mask
of their general critique of power politics. What saved them from blind
crusading was that they did not dwell in the world of abstraction for
too long. They always returned to everyday reality and concrete political issues. Their critique of power never became their ultimate objective but remained a tool with which they analyzed actual political
problems.

For the realists, analyzing power and power relationships was a way
to deal both with the brute realities of the political world and with their

1. Charles A. McClelland, *Theory and the International System* (New York, 1966), 82.

own ideas of how the world *should* be. Such analysis was a way of reconciling the real with the ideal; it provided a method by which the realists could comment on the ethical dimensions of political problems without lapsing into either pure idealism or pure cynicism. Power and power relationships are entities that can be felt keenly. They can be terrifyingly real—as in the case of nuclear weapons—and they are easily recognizable. Everyone in every conceivable walk of life is affected by power relationships, whether these be military, economic, or merely familial. The realists seemed to understand this, and they naturally gravitated toward the concept of power as the subject of their work.

Implicit in their analyses of power, however, was a "calendar of values," a set of assumptions that acted as their moral guide to the political world. This guide was never codified into dogma or doctrine; instead, it remained rather loosely defined as a collection of principles. The realists never espoused a specific, unchanging code of morality for power politics. What they did offer was a general approach to—and a way of seeing—the ethical aspects of practical political issues.[2]

It was natural that power became a central theme for writers of political philosophy and political commentary in postwar America. Never in history had a nation had so much power at its disposal. Following the war the United States possessed preeminent political, military, and economic power—power that made the nation's previous status as an important force in international affairs look relatively minor. Unschooled and inexperienced in the role of world leader and superpower, the United States found itself needing to learn its new part in a hurry. Niebuhr's words of 1932 were more appropriate than ever in 1945: "The political situation and problem of America in world affairs can be put in one sentence: America is at once the most powerful and politically the most ignorant of modern nations."[3]

2. For more on realism as an "approach" rather than as a "tight doctrine," see Charles Frankel, "Morality and U.S. Foreign Policy," *Worldview,* XVIII (June, 1975), 13–23. Frankel also discusses the importance of the concept of the national interest. He argues that in determining the national interest, the realists establish their "calendar of values."

3. Reinhold Niebuhr, "Perils of American Power," *Atlantic,* CXLIX (January, 1932), 90.

The major questions facing the United States concerned what to do with its newly found power. Would the American people insist on a return to isolation? Would they, in the words of Averell Harriman, be content to "go to the movies and drink Coke"? Or would they opt for a more ambitious role for themselves and the nation? The answers of course would vary, although the sentiments expressed in Kennan's "X" article, the Truman Doctrine, and the Marshall Plan gave clear indications of which way the government was leaning.

Most important, however, was a strong sense within the government and the nation as a whole that along with power came responsibility. Responsibility, in this context, was a concept that cut two ways. In one sense, responsibility meant obligations to others—for example, to the NATO allies. In another sense, responsibility referred to the obligations that Americans felt they had to themselves and to their ideals— meaning, among other things, that power must be used in ways that Americans themselves deemed responsible. This latter point was illustrated most clearly, perhaps, in the realist critique of nuclear-weapons policies. The atomic bomb was, after all, the ultimate symbol of American power and hegemony. Along with the privileges the weapon bestowed upon its owners, it brought the burden of responsibility.

Defining Power: The Issue Is Control

Like realism, power is a slippery concept, difficult to pin down. Yet the realists were undeterred by its elusiveness and the difficulties inherent in attempting to define it. They made pursuit of its meaning central to their work, using a variety of formulas, metaphors, and literary devices to explain it.

At the most basic level, power implies strength and the ability to accomplish a task. It is performance-oriented; that is, it is calculated by its potential to achieve certain results. It is also descriptive in that it usually refers to a relationship between forces or things. In fact, power means nothing by itself; it must refer to a relationship between two or more entities. When thus generalized in terms of strength, force, and relationships between entities, the concept of power remains a rather abstract one. When it is applied to real situations, however, it can shed light on the most substantive of issues.

It was in its application to real situations that the concept of power interested the realists. Further, power seemed to them most meaningful when expressed in terms of one of its subdivisions, such as political, military, or economic power. For example, a realist was more likely to speak of a certain type of power, such as military power, than to talk about "power" in general. The use of subdivisions added both depth and accuracy to the realists' use of the concept. By sticking to their preferred subdivisions and avoiding references to a flat, generic concept of power, the realists succeeded in making the analysis of power a useful tool for the study of world affairs.

"When we speak of power," wrote Morgenthau, "we mean man's control over the minds and actions of other men." To have power, according to Morgenthau, is to have control. Naturally, "all nations want to either keep power, increase power, or demonstrate power"; and every nation bases its foreign policy on an estimate of its own power in relation to that of its competitors.[4] Every nation wants complete control of its destiny (and sometimes the destiny of others). Morgenthau knew that complete control over destiny is impossible, but he argued for maintaining as much control as possible. He had concluded that it is better to control one's own destiny than to leave it to the whims of others. From Morgenthau's perspective, all the machinations of states—all of their actions, statements, and rhetoric—are directly related to the all-important struggle for power and control. Almost nothing is done without the ultimate goal in mind: to increase the power of one's own nation and therefore increase its security.

Raw power, Morgenthau realized, is not always directly convertible to control: strength does not necessarily lead to mastery. Morgenthau knew that power that did not enhance control was useless. In his view, the only useful power was power that could be made to serve specific ends. Therefore, Morgenthau measured power by its relative ability to

4. Morgenthau, *Politics Among Nations: The Struggle for Power and Peace* (New York, 1948), 13–18.

control "the minds and actions of other men." Forms of power that were not related to the object of control had little interest for him.

This critique of power had very specific applications. At the heart of it lay the distinction between usable and unusable power, a theme of timely significance in the wake of the mass destruction caused by both the conventional and atomic bombings of World War II. Most important, however, was the vital distinction that provided the framework for all discussion on these issues—the distinction between *political* and *military* power.

Morgenthau insisted that political power denoted only "the mutual relations of control among the holders of public authority . . . and the people at large." Military power implied "the actual exercise of physical violence." When force is used, he wrote, "it signifies the abdication of political power in favor of military or pseudo-military power."[5] Morgenthau was wary of the use of military power because it was so difficult to calculate its effects. Military power often was employed as a last resort, when all else had failed, and usually by a nation desperate to establish itself or reassert its position. The very uncertainties inherent in the use of force made it hazardous. If the ultimate purpose of power was to gain control, then the use of physical power or force to achieve that purpose was suspect at best.

Distinctions between political and military power are difficult to maintain. In some instances, the realists were hard-pressed to sustain their argument that there is a very real difference between the two. The most notable example of this difficulty was the previously mentioned case of Kennan and his notion of containment. Kennan maintains to this day that he used the term *containment* to refer to an "ideological-political" problem; he never meant for it to be interpreted—as Lippmann did in 1947—as a "military" doctrine.[6] Unfortunately for Kennan, few Americans seemed intellectually dextrous enough or emotionally willing to grant him this distinction. Countless policy makers and political analysts assumed that containment referred to military

5. *Ibid.*, 13–14.
6. See, for example, George Kennan, "Containment Then and Now," *Foreign Affairs,* LXV (Spring, 1987), 885–90.

41

obligations. Why Kennan was so misunderstood is open for debate. Whatever the reason, it is evident that the realist distinction between political and military power was lost on practically everyone except the realists themselves.

This difficulty is noteworthy because it points to the place where realism comes under stress, revealing its inner workings. The category of military power—and more specifically the use of force—compelled the realists to stretch their philosophy of power to its limits. For that reason, the realists' treatment of the subdivision of military power warrants a close look, especially as regards such power's most troublesome and challenging aspect: the presence of nuclear weapons in the nation's arsenal.

Responsible Power

In one of his first professional writings to be published in the United States, Morgenthau suggested that it is the task of every generation "to rediscover and reformulate the perennial problems of political ethics and to answer them in the light of the experience of the age." [7] Virtually every realist held a similar view. Unfortunately for Morgenthau and his colleagues, it fell to their generation to address the classic problems of political ethics under the shadow of the atomic bomb. Yet in meeting the challenge of this task, the realists did some of their finest work. They were not shaken by the new dimension that nuclear weapons added to the classic questions. To deal with these unprecedented developments, the realists went back to their own philosophical roots. Dusting off an age-old realist notion, they began to rely on what can be called the concept of responsible power.

Responsible power, as the realists constructed it, highlighted *judgment* and *accountability*. It leaned toward utilitarianism, emphasizing practical results as its standard of judgment. Like the utilitarians, the realists generally favored policies designed to provide "the greatest happiness to the greatest number." The realists, however, did not fol-

7. Hans Morgenthau, "The Evil of Politics and the Ethics of Evil," *Ethics,* LVI (October, 1945), 1.

low the utilitarian path to its logical extreme; they maintained—forcefully at times—that the "greatest good" yardstick was in some cases far from the last word. As perceptions of power changed, the realists were able to adapt. Their ideas about responsibility and what constituted the responsible use of power were tied inextricably to the prevailing perception of power itself.

The realist concept of responsible power owed much to the work of Max Weber, one of the intellectual fathers of modern realism and a particular favorite of Morgenthau. It was Weber, in his essay "Politics as a Vocation," who outlined the central problem of political ethics that concerned the realists. This problem (as Weber presented it) was one of balancing the tension between "ethics" and "politics"; Weber's essay was in essence an investigation of the oxymoronic phrase "political ethics." He concluded that two standards of morality exist: one for the ideal world and one for the real world—the world of politics. Neither standard is superior to the other, but each is appropriate to its own realm: ideal standards must hold for the ideal realm, and pragmatic standards must hold for the political realm. The key to a successful life in politics, according to Weber, was not to confuse the two realms.[8]

Weber's model of ethical dualism was based on maintaining this distinction between ethics and politics. "Ethics" deals with the way the world *ought* to be, "politics" with the way it *is*. Weber expressed this duality with two phrases that, used together, illustrate the paradox of "political ethics." The first phrase is "ethic of ultimate ends." It refers to intention, and it holds that *intent* is the most important factor in considering the moral dimension of an action. Therefore, a person subscribing to the ethic of ultimate ends would have less regard for the actual consequences of his action than for its intended effect. Opposed to this ethic is the "ethic of responsibility." This phrase refers to consequences and implies that the morality of an act is related directly to the *results* that stem from it. Intent is secondary. A person subscribing to the ethic of responsibility would judge the morality of an act by the outcome it produces.

8. See Max Weber, "Politics as a Vocation," in H. H. Gerth and C. Wright Mills, eds., *From Max Weber: Essays in Sociology* (New York, 1958), 77–128.

By juxtaposing the ethic of ultimate ends and the ethic of responsibility, Weber set up the classic paradox found at the heart of any discussion of morality and politics. Moreover, he provided the vocabulary and phrasing for some of the most vexing questions a political philosopher can ask. Is intent a justifiable standard of moral judgment even if the results of an action prove disastrous? What if the results of an action turn out to be satisfactory even though the original goal was less than ideal? Finally, Weber raised the issue of statesmanship. Who is the more desirable political actor, he asked, the person guided by the ethic of ultimate ends or the person guided by the ethic of responsibility?

Weber, like most political realists, was very much at home with paradox. At times he seemed to revel in it. His greatest achievement, in fact, was in illuminating paradoxes and making them accessible to those who could benefit from their explication. He went to painstaking lengths to display the strengths and weaknesses of both his "ethics" before venturing an assessment. Then, like most thinkers who recognize paradox, Weber remained somewhere between the extremes he had outlined. Refusing to endorse either ethic, he urged a blending of the two and contended that "an ethic of ultimate ends and an ethic of responsibility are not absolute contrasts but rather supplements, which only in unison can constitute a genuine man—a man who *can* have the 'calling for politics'"

"Politics as a Vocation" can be read as a sermon to the politically ambitious. Among Weber's purposes was to warn those who would enter the political arena that they should not expect to emerge from it unscathed. Good intentions—the ethic of ultimate ends—will not suffice to protect them, for this ethic "cannot stand up to the ethical irrationality of the world." Nor will pure pragmatism be the answer: Weber alerted the uninitiated to the fact that there is another realm besides the pragmatic, and that they would do well to consider it. "Politics," he declared, "is a strong and slow boring of hard boards. It takes both passion and perspective."[9]

9. *Ibid.*, 127, 122, 128.

According to Weber, the ideal political actor is aware of the ethical paradoxes facing him and yet remains willing to act. He has vision and noble intent, but he also is aware of the practical consequences of his actions. He recognizes that noble ends and noble means do not always coincide. Sometimes, tragically, in pursuit of noble ends a statesman might have to engage in what he normally would consider to be immoral activity. Because he is responsible to his constituents and must take action that will produce consequences favorable to them, he cannot afford the luxury of idealism. The life of a worthy politician is filled with moral anguish. Weber's message to politicians is that they must be prepared to get their hands dirty. Politics is no place for someone who wishes to remain pure.

In separating the "ethical" from the "political," Weber and the realists did not mean to suggest that these realms had nothing to do with each other; on the contrary, they insisted that each was vitally relevant to the other. The problem, as the realists saw it, was the confusion that resulted from the careless mixing of the two realms. Such sloppiness led to the muddled thinking that was all too common in political debate. The realists never intended to separate the two realms and keep them separated; that is, they never expected to deny the ethical dimensions of political actions or the political dimensions of ethical positions. What they did promote was a clear articulation of the issues in both realms, followed by a careful attempt to join the two together. This approach, the realists believed, would free them from illusions, and in following it, they eventually developed a pattern of analysis. In its finished form, this pattern gave shape to the concept of responsible power—a concept sensitive to both ultimate ends (intentions) and responsibility (consequences).

In the end, the Weberian scheme actually formalized the rejection of a dual standard of morality. Machiavellian notions of raison d'état were dismissed: actions taken on behalf of the state were not justified automatically. Although the realists were sympathetic to the plight of the statesman who had to make hard decisions in a Hobbesian world where life was "solitary, poor, nasty, brutish, and short," they held that these conditions did not give him carte blanche in the conduct of his affairs. The statesman was always morally accountable even though he faced pressures that the private citizen did not.

In seeking to render moral assessments of the actions of the statesman while taking into account his special circumstances, the realists developed the notion of a moral continuum. The continuum left room for the Niebuhrian idea of "moral man and immoral society"—that is, that there are inescapable differences between public and private morality. Significantly, however, despite acknowledging these clear differences, the moral continuum did not allow for public and private morality to be measured on different scales. The continuum allowed for the fact that the public man, acting on behalf of the state, would engage in activities that he would never pursue in his private affairs—but this fact did not absolve him from scrutiny according to a unified scale of judgment.

Much of this thinking was brought to bear at Nuremberg. War criminals whose defense was that they had acted on behalf of the state—fulfilling their duty as public men—found little sympathy among the realists. The use of "duty" as an excuse for amoral and immoral behavior was galling and unacceptable. The realists would wrestle with this problem, as embodied in the notion of the continuum, for the rest of their careers. Later, the "duty" of a statesman to threaten massive destruction, if not annihilation, with nuclear weapons was particularly troubling. Clearly, by virtue of his duty to defend the state, the statesman was required to do all that he could to insure its survival. But did this duty really include such terrible threats? And could such a problem possibly be gauged on any continuum?

A key point for the realists was that the Weberian system of assessing such problems did not allow for the suspension or even the radical revision of moral judgment. The statesman, like the private citizen, was expected to do his best to uphold the moral principles venerated by society. Along with the idea of "interest defined as power," these moral principles were essential guideposts to the statesman seeking to navigate through difficult dilemmas. In emphasizing the link between public and private morality, the realists made it clear that for the statesman, neither could stand on its own.

Ironically, the realists' obsession with clarity has led to generations of confusion. The realists consistently have been misread and misinterpreted, and many critics have dismissed them as amoral advocates of power politics. Critics have taken the realists' insistence on maintaining the separation between "ethics" and "politics" to mean that the realists saw no place for morality as a standard of judgment in international relations; similarly, the realists' concept of the moral continuum has been seen as an affirmation of a dual standard of morality. In both cases, nothing could be farther from the truth. The realists' main concern about morality in international relations was that "good intentions" not become the sole factor or even an especially prominent factor in the making of policy decisions. They warned against pursuing desirable moral goals at the risk of disastrous political results. And they never subscribed to any kind of dual standard of morality.

In his 1973 article "Moral Skepticism and International Relations," the philosopher Marshall Cohen joined a long line of critics who have accused the realists of abandoning morality as a standard of judgment in international relations in favor of a crude notion of power politics.[10] He criticized the postwar realists for throwing out the good with the bad when they, in his words, "(feel) compelled to adopt the untenable position that international conduct cannot and should not be judged by moral standards."[11] Cohen granted that the realists may have been correct when they stated that moralistic-legalistic attitudes can have "a pernicious influence on foreign policy," but he adamantly maintained that morality itself must play some role in the decision-making process. Arguing against what he saw as the moral skepticism of the realists, Cohen concluded that international conduct must be open to moral assessment.

In making his argument, Cohen did a disservice to the realists. His one-dimensional treatment of them leaves him open to the charge that he used the realists as straw men whom he introduced only to discredit. Cohen painted the realists as advocates of the narrow idea that "the

10. Marshall Cohen, "Moral Skepticism and International Relations," *Philosophy and Public Affairs*, XIII (Fall, 1984), 299–346.
11. *Ibid.*, 305.

conduct of nations is, and should be, guided and judged exclusively by the amoral requirements of the national interest." He proceeded to argue that the realists had "an overly simple conception of the structure of morality" that was in fact no different from that of "the moralists who are the main subject of their attack."

Cohen's reductionist caricature obscured the true depth and complexity of realism. To say that the realists favored policies guided by the "amoral requirements of the national interest" is to miss the point of realism entirely. The realists would have found the very phrase "amoral requirements of the national interest" nonsensical because, to their way of thinking, national interest was by definition closely tied to morality. Implicit in their idea of national interest was a commitment to righteousness and proper moral behavior. If the realists judged national interest in terms of power (and they did), it was *responsible* power—power considered in relation to its possible political and ethical ramifications.

In arguing against the realists, Cohen, perhaps unwittingly, was attacking a group whose beliefs were not far from his own. Although the realists were moral skeptics of a certain stripe, they were actually closer to the "complex moralists" whom Cohen discussed (and seemed to admire) than to the caricature he presented at the beginning of the article. For all their talk of power politics, the realists never suggested an amoral approach to international affairs. Cohen acknowledged this and even cited some examples of Morgenthau's statements to the same effect. Yet for some reason, perhaps to satisfy his need to enhance the glitter of his arguments, Cohen made the realists appear to be more skeptical than they were.

The point of Cohen's article was that international conduct should be open to moral assessment. Ironically, the realists would have agreed wholeheartedly. They knew that policies that failed to take moral considerations into account would have little support at home and little respect abroad. The only point over which the realists might have differed with Cohen was the one of priority; that is, they might have disagreed with his idea of the *extent* to which moral arguments should provide the basis and impetus for foreign policy. Beyond that, however,

Cohen himself sounded like a postwar realist when he wrote that "the way of life we are defending is founded on moral principles that are plainly incompatible with the amoral pursuit of power." He went on to state that "the unrestrained pursuit of power will be condemned by the moral principles we ourselves acknowledge."[12] Hans Morgenthau could not have said it better himself.

The convergence of Cohen and Morgenthau was not accidental; both took power and morality to be inseparable. Responsible power as the realists conceived it took into account two realms: the ethical (the ideal) and the political (the real). It recognized that political actors have allegiances to both realms and that, inevitably, choices must be made between the two. Above all, responsible power called for statesmanship; it was the statesman who had to make it work. Facing morally ambiguous situations, the statesman exercised responsible power by making pragmatic choices without ignoring the moral dimension of his decisions.

In addition, responsible power implied consensus. That is, it required that there be an agreed-upon set of principles, a body of values and goals that could act as the statesman's moral compass. These principles most likely were attainable only in the ideal realm; nevertheless, they could give direction to the statesman who had to act in the political realm. Responsible power derived its meaning from what the statesman was responsible *to*. In other words, the concept hinged on the question, To what principles is the statesman being held accountable?

A statesman working within the constraints of responsible power would be particularly sensitive to the principles agreed upon in the consensus. These principles would represent a "vital center," a place where the diverse interests of the body politic were unified. No statesman who considered himself a true representative of his constituents could fail to pay heed to the consensus—assuming, of course, that he could find it.

Finally, responsible power implied criticism. Indeed, it was criticism that made consensus meaningful. Only after criticism clarified the

12. *Ibid.*, 309.

principles embodied in consensus could commitment to them become solidified. Criticism also kept responsible power "clean": an endless tinkering with the notion of responsibility insured that power would not be thought of in purely partisan or political terms, but would remain forever wedded to a consensual view of what constituted responsibility. This dialectic between criticism and consensus, if used appropriately, not only made responsible power fluid enough to be responsive to the ever-changing nuances of the consensus, but at the same time provided a relatively stable model of what responsible power should be.

The acknowledgment of the creative and practical aspects of this dialectic was one of realism's most attractive features. In essence, the dialectic produced a model that outlined the possibilities for moral action. It made clear the specific values that were to be served by responsible power, and it suggested practical steps and useful structures to encourage the achievement of such power. For the realists, the values that emerged from this dialectic included prudence, humility, the good-faith effort to balance ideals and self-interests, and the preservation of freedom as expressed in the idea of democracy. These values came to constitute the model of responsible power that realism promoted.

By calling for the constant critical evaluation of power, the realists avoided one of power's worst by-products: intoxication. Responsible power did not allow the blind assumption that power is inherently good or desirable. It always asked, Power employed toward what end? The concept of responsible power enabled the realists to challenge popular postwar presumptions of American moral and military superiority. It allowed them to cut through the haughty attitudes of the day, and it provided them with the vocabulary they needed to speak effectively about power and humility.

Responsible power was offered as a corrective to what Niebuhr termed "an uncritical reverence for the supposed wisdom of the American way of life" and the belief that "our power is the natural fruit of our virtue." [13] This corrective did not always prevail, but it loomed

13. Reinhold Niebuhr, "American Pride and Power," *American Scholar*, XVII (Autumn, 1948), 393–94.

large in the realists' reservations regarding interventions in the third world—especially in their opposition to the war in Vietnam. In any case, to the realists responsible power was bigger than the moment or the particular problem in question; it was based on a grander scale: that of civilization. At its best, responsible power provided three things: criticism, a quest for consensus, and a recognition of the statesman's dilemma. Considered in its overall cultural context, it can best be understood as a logical outgrowth of the quest for a "public philosophy."

The Public Philosophy: A Search for Consensus

Responsible power is a viable concept only if there is an agreed-upon set of principles as to what constitutes responsible behavior. In a pluralistic society such as the United States, it can be difficult to reach any agreement on principles, let alone maintain a consensus. The postwar era, however, celebrated consensus; it was a time when many intellectuals argued that the story of America was one of consensus rather than conflict. The realists were no exception; they believed that there was indeed a latent consensus—a public philosophy—present in American society, a consensus that embodied the best traditions and values of Western civilization.

The realists' task, as they saw it, was to revive and renew the public philosophy. Their mission was to update it and make it known to community leaders. In doing so, they would uncover and make explicit the consensus of basic values that held together the American community. The work that spearheaded this realist activity was Walter Lippmann's *Essays in the Public Philosophy* (1955). It not only provided a name for the endeavor, but also presented a clear explanation of the term itself.

According to Lippmann, the public philosophy as it existed in history was a "doctrine of natural law, which held that there was a law 'above the ruler and sovereign people . . . above the whole community of mortals.'" Paraphrasing the classical Stoic thinker Zeno, Lippmann suggested that "a large plural society cannot be governed without recognizing that transcending its plural interests, there is a rational order with a superior common law. This common law is 'natural' in the sense

51

that it can be discovered in any rational mind." In a society where this natural law held sway, it would follow that there be "a rational order of things in which it is possible, by sincere inquiry and rational debate, to distinguish the true and the false, the right and the wrong, the good which leads to the realization of human ends and the evil which leads to destruction and to the death of civility." [14]

The problem, as Lippmann saw it, lay in making the tradition of public philosophy speak to the modern age and to a new generation. "The school of natural law," he declared, "has not been able to cope with the pluralism of the later modern age—with the pluralism which has resulted from the industrial revolution and from the enfranchisement and the emancipation of the masses of people." It remained for the public philosopher to make tradition relevant to modern problems: to "re-establish confidence in the validity of public standards" and to "renew the convictions from which our political morality springs." [15] Lippmann continually stressed his opinion that the public philosophy did not have to be "discovered or invented": "It is known," he said. "The poignant question is whether, and if so, how modern men [can] make vital contact with the lost traditions of civility." [16]

Lippmann's entire concept of a public philosophy was based on the assumption that there was in fact a consensus "out there" in the body politic, and that it only needed to be articulated, nurtured, and perhaps slightly reworked for the modern age. "When the adherence of the whole body of people to the public philosophy is firm," he wrote, "a true community exists; when there is division and dissent over the main principles the result is a condition of latent war." [17] He wanted to restore a strong sense of community in America by elucidating the working consensus embodied in the public philosophy.

Lippmann understood the forces of entropy that were all too evident in modern life: unabated urbanization, overwhelming technolog-

14. Lippmann, *Essays in the Public Philosophy,* (Boston, 1955), 97, 106–107, 134, 109–14, 102.
15. *Ibid.,* 109–114.
16. *Ibid.,* 102.
17. *Ibid.,* 134.

ical change, and the growing influence of mass culture. He believed that American democracy was showing the same signs of weakness visible in the other Western democracies: its pluralism was turning into the abject pluralism of other liberal states—states that had been transformed into paralytic "mass democracies." Yet in the face of this entropy Lippmann had faith in a higher order, one wherein the cohesiveness of Western civilization was affirmed—and wherein the public philosophy reigned supreme. It was here that the claims of "contradictory and competing private worlds" would be settled in accord with a sovereign "public world."

Essays in the Public Philosophy echoed the work of Weber. Like Weber, Lippmann posited the existence of two realms, one belonging to the "real," the other to the "ideal." The "realm of existence" is the world of everyday life; it is where man works, struggles, and lives out his bodily existence. The "realm of essence" is the world of the spirit; it is the transcendent world of souls. Also like Weber, Lippmann warned that "the root of all error is in the confusion of the two realms." It is "the radical error of the modern democratic gospel," he wrote, "that it promises not the good life of this world but the perfect life of heaven." This faulty perspective "inhibits the good life of this world" and "falsifies the life of the spirit." [18]

Lippmann's purpose in defining two realms and establishing their characteristics was similar to Weber's. Although he made a sincere effort to establish the distinction between the two realms, he denied their ultimate autonomy. Neither realm can stand on its own, for all people have body and soul; all live with both the real and the ideal. It is important not to mistake one realm for the other, and equally important to maintain some sort of balance between the realms. This balance is precarious and ever-shifting. Merely finding it is a challenge, maintaining it even more difficult. But it is in this process of finding the balance that man makes his moral stand. In that gray area, Lippmann believed, man makes decisions that define him as a moral being.

Lippmann's sternest warning was also similar to Weber's: those who

---

18. *Ibid.*, 142.

failed to recognize the distinction between the two realms were politically dangerous. Such men, Lippmann claimed, were the ones causing the destruction of the public philosophy. They were feeding the confusion already reigning in the weakened Western democracies. The public philosophy, as he conceived of it, would be an antidote for these men's one-dimensional thought. It would become the new standard for the nation's political morality.

By guarding against the twin perils of moral absolutism and moral relativism, the public philosopher would insure that neither became dominant. Lippmann maintained that only through the active cultivation of the public philosophy could the two realms be rendered useful for political purposes. When used appropriately, the public philosophy would endow terms such as *democracy, freedom, order,* and *personal integrity* with real meaning.[19] In this way the public philosopher would be an important political actor, conversing in both realms with the goal of establishing a viable code of political morality.

The ultimate purpose of the public philosophy was to establish "a common faith" for the American people. This faith would provide guidelines and principles with which leaders could help the nation solve its political and moral problems, as well as strengthen its resolve. Even the intellectual archrival of the realists, John Dewey—from whom Lippmann borrowed the phrase "a common faith"—realized the need for a public philosophy. Dewey's conclusion to *A Common Faith* (1934) easily could be mistaken for an excerpt from Lippmann's *Public Philosophy:* "Ours is the responsibility of conserving, transmitting, rectifying and expanding the heritage of values we have received that those who come after us may receive it more solid and secure, more widely accessible and more generously shared than we have received it. Here are all the elements for a religious faith that shall not be confined to sect, class or race. Such a faith has always been implicitly the common faith of mankind. It remains to make it explicit and militant."[20] Dewey's emphasis, like Lippmann's, was on continuity.

19. See Charles Wellborn, *Twentieth-Century Pilgrimage: Walter Lippmann and the Public Philosophy* (Baton Rouge, 1969), 159.

20. John Dewey, *A Common Faith* (New Haven, 1934), 87.

Understanding his life and experiences as one link in the great chain of civilization, he too made sense of things by the way they related to a grander scheme. Dewey saw himself as both conservator and educator. He took it upon himself to conserve the heritage of values he had received, as well as to clarify them and make them known to his contemporaries.

Dewey's differences with the realists—most notably Niebuhr—were related more to methods than to substance. When Dewey's disciple Morton White waged his well-known, full-frontal attack on Lippmann and Niebuhr in the 1957 edition of *Social Thought in America*, his main points of assault were Niebuhr's Hegelianism and insistence on Original Sin, and Lippmann's nebulous conception of natural law. In opposition to the doctrines of Original Sin and natural law, White offered a more scientific approach: instrumentalism.[21] But White's Deweyan instrumentalism, for all its emphasis on scientific analysis and empiricism, was pursued with the same end in mind as Niebuhr's Hegelianism or Lippmann's natural law. What was at stake was a consensus on moral reasoning. Whatever one might call it—a "common faith," the "public philosophy," or "Christian realism"—the outcome was similar. Instrumentalism was based on scientific analysis and progress, whereas Christian realism and natural law were based on history and tradition. But all three systems were geared toward the same end: to build a cohesive sense of political morality based on recognizable moral principles.

Dewey, Niebuhr, Lippmann, and White all were engaged in an effort to apply philosophy to public affairs. All of them took a broad view of the enterprise they were pursuing. White may have expressed it best when he stated his belief that "a philosopher may fruitfully unite an interest in logical analysis with one in the history of ideas and another in what is sometimes called cultural criticism." In any case, these pub-

21. See Morton White, *Social Thought in America: The Revolt Against Formalism* (Rev. ed.; New York, 1957). This book was first published in 1949, but White's most telling attack did not appear until 1957. See the preface to the 1957 edition for his comments on Lippmann and Niebuhr. (This preface is included in subsequent editions of the book).

lic philosophers' real concerns centered less on the nuances of analytic philosophy than on how philosophy could illuminate other disciplines and the culture at large. They were "bridge builders" hoping to "contribute to the resolution or clarification of fundamental problems of civilized life."[22] All of them used analytic philosophy (albeit with varying degrees of sophistication), but principally as just another tool with which to pursue their primary goal of cultural criticism.

The cultural problems the public philosophers most often addressed were those featured most prominently in Lippmann's book: the decline of the West, the fate of liberalism in the modern age, and the question of pluralism. The problem of pluralism, in fact, was at the root of the realists' unease. Conventional wisdom has it that the very term *pluralism* implies an underlying consensus of values that provides a foundation on which differing but compatible views can stand. The realists accepted this premise but feared that the special conditions of the postwar world might have invalidated it. Where, they wondered, was "the unifying ideology, faith, or myth" that was needed to provide the foundation for their plural society? How, "amid the multiplying claims for status and power," would they be able to "revitalize a common faith" that would serve to arbitrate between the warring factions within the culture?[23] The realists were worried about the deterioration of national unity and the possible failure of national will. In a world where totalitarianism stood as the implacable foe, paralysis—whether caused by political and cultural factionalism or by the lethargy of a directionless mass society—was exceedingly dangerous.

Lippmann believed that the solutions to these problems could come from within American culture itself. That an old, dormant consensus

22. Morton White, *Pragmatism and the American Mind: Essays and Reviews in Philosophy and Intellectual History* (New York, 1973), preface.
23. See John Higham, *Send These to Me: Jews and Other Immigrants in Urban America* (New York, 1975), esp. chap. 10, "Ethnic Pluralism in Modern American Thought," and chap. 11, "Another American Dilemma." Although not himself a realist public philosopher of the kind discussed here, John Higham is an authority on the subject of pluralism and consensus.

existed within the mainstream of American culture Lippmann had no doubt; that it was in danger, he was equally sure. But in insisting that the consensus could be recovered and made useful, Lippmann, like other American public philosophers, was asserting that unity was possible. His quest—like Dewey's before it—for a new secular expression of political morality revealed his faith in Western values. It also revealed his belief that those values could play a positive role in meeting the challenges presented by both the external menace of Communism and the possibility of internal collapse.

Looked at in this way, Lippmann's articulation of the public philosophy can be seen as a unique product of its time. Although it was a logical extension of an American tradition stretching back through the mugwumps and at least as far as Jefferson, it was also an apt symbol for the intellectual state of America in the 1940s and 1950s. In grappling with the issues of pluralism, consensus, and political will, Lippmann's quest for the public philosophy epitomized the political, moral, and spiritual concerns facing postwar America.

The parallels between Lippmann's work and that of the "consensus intellectuals" (especially the "consensus historians") who dominated the intellectual landscape of the era are readily apparent. Like the consensus historians, Lippmann emphasized consensus over conflict, continuity over disruption. Richard Hofstadter, in *The American Political Tradition* (1948) and *The Age of Reform* (1955); Louis Hartz, in *The Liberal Tradition in America* (1955); and Daniel Boorstin, in *The Genius of American Politics* (1953), set the tone for their generation of historians. Opposing their work to that of the so-called progressive historians— Charles Beard, Vernon L. Parrington, and Frederick Jackson Turner— who preceded them, the consensus historians concentrated their studies on the beliefs and values that Americans shared rather than on those that divided them.[24]

The consensus school gained notoriety when John Higham iden-

24. For an excellent summary of the intellectual climate described here, see Richard Pells, *The Liberal Mind in a Conservative Age: American Intellectuals in the 1940s and 1950s* (New York, 1985), esp. 147–62.

tified it in an article he wrote for *Commentary* in 1959.[25] "The Cult of the 'American Consensus'" received much attention, in part because it was one of the first attempts to analyze the new style of historical scholarship as a "movement," and in part because it offered some sharp criticisms of that style. In some subsequent commentaries on the consensus school, a revisionist argument of some merit has been developed. Whether one subscribes to Higham's original view or to the revisionist line of thinking, however, it is safe to say that Lippmann's *Public Philosophy* fits the consensus mold.

Higham argued that the "new look" of American history was "strikingly conservative." More than at any time before, he claimed, "historians are discovering a placid and unexciting past." He accused his colleagues of "carrying out a massive grading operation to smooth over America's social convulsions." The result, he concluded, was that the new contemporary conservatism had "a deadening effect on the historian's ability to take a conflict of ideas seriously." It is not hard to see Lippmann's book in this context. Like Hofstadter, Hartz, and Boorstin, Lippmann assumed that a certain homogeneity and conformity existed in American society and that it could be made visible through the study of history. Lippmann's public philosophy suggested that there is a place where theologians and scientists, liberals and conservatives, can meet and agree. The messier aspects of democracy—the bellowing masses and the pesky special interests—he discussed only with disdain.

The revisionists have been more generous than Higham in assessing the qualities of the consensus school, and they have revealed another side to it. Most important, they have shown that the consensus historians did not focus on consensus and consensus only. Revisionists such as Richard Pells, Daniel J. Singal, and Richard Gillam have pointed out the "critical ideal" present within the consensus historians' work.[26] They have argued that far from being undiscerning celebrants

25. John Higham, "The Cult of the 'American Consensus,'" *Commentary*, XXVII (February, 1959), 93–100.

26. See Pells, *Liberal Mind in a Conservative Age;* Daniel J. Singal, "Beyond Consensus: Richard Hofstadter and American Historiography," *American Historical Review*, LXXXIX (October, 1984), 976–1004; and Richard Gillam, "Richard Hofstadter, C.

of American culture, the consensus historians were in fact quite critical of pervasive American values and looked at the past with anything but nostalgia. The consensus school admired the special qualities of America as a nation but did not pass up chances to probe its shortcomings. For example, Hofstadter's *The American Political Tradition* "is one of the most jaundiced views of American political history ever written by a major scholar," according to Singal. "That it sold so well for so long (over one million copies) and was adopted as a textbook by thousands of college and high school students is surely an irony."[27]

The revisionists have proved that the consensus era was not one of blind affirmation, but of a search for the roots of the values that had come to be accepted and even exalted in American society. The search was the antithesis of simple historical exposition; it involved complex cultural analysis. That the consensus historians were interdisciplinary thinkers, well versed in almost all of the social sciences, was no coincidence. Historians such as Hofstadter and Hartz used the tools of history, psychology, political science, sociology, and literary analysis in writing their works of "history." In essence, much like Lippmann and the other realists, they were cultural critics—and the word *critics* should be reemphasized. The consensus historians produced criticisms of American culture that were more opposed to the mainstream than often is realized.

Again, it is not hard to place Lippmann's *Public Philosophy* within the context of the consensus philosophy, even given the revisionist reformulation of that philosophy. In fact, the revisionist argument may reveal the connection between the two more clearly by calling attention to both sides of the era of consensus: affirmation *and* criticism. *The Public Philosophy* was an affirmation of the Western and American cultural heritage *and* a jeremiad regarding America's cultural health. Lippmann both proclaimed the potential strength of tradition and lamented its neglect. *The Public Philosophy* was also a call to arms, an

---

Wright Mills, and 'the Critical Ideal,'" *American Scholar,* XLVII (Winter, 1977–78), 69–85.

27. Singal, "Beyond Consensus," 983.

urgent appeal for the restoration of consensus, community, and the will to act. In no way could it be construed as the work of a reposed thinker content to celebrate the status quo.

One of the foundation texts of the consensus school was Arthur Schlesinger, Jr.'s *The Vital Center* (1949). It is useful to look at *The Public Philosophy* in the light of this book, which forcefully and simply describes how Schlesinger and many of his contemporaries understood the challenges facing them in the postwar world. Indeed, *The Public Philosophy* (and the work of the consensus historians) can be viewed as a response to Schlesinger.

Wary of the threat of communism and the lure of totalitarianism, Schlesinger urged his colleagues and fellow citizens to forge a consensus—a vital center—in order to meet and defeat the ideological foe. Exposing the historical failures of both the American Left and Right, Schlesinger illustrated their weaknesses while laying the groundwork for what he hoped would be a new approach to politics. Portraying totalitarianism as the worst of all enemies, he argued that the task before American society was to perpetuate personal freedom while also providing "a sense of belonging" for all individuals. "We must somehow give the lonely masses a sense of individual human function," he proclaimed. "We must restore community to the political order." In conclusion, Schlesinger suggested that a new radicalism should emerge, one whose object was "to reunite the individual and the community in a fruitful union." [28]

In *The Public Philosophy*, Lippmann tried to do all that and more. He sought to transcend categories of Left and Right; he attempted to give a renewed sense of purpose to the individual living in a mass society; above all, he strove to revive a sense of community—as well as the values and obligations that the idea of "community" demands—among American citizens. His book did not merely complement Schlesinger's concept of a vital center; it embodied it. As a piece of cultural criticism aiming toward consensus, it could not have been

28. Arthur Schlesinger, Jr., *The Vital Center: The Politics of Freedom* (Rev. ed.; Boston, 1962), 247, 255–56.

more representative of its era. As a call to action for fear of social collapse, however, it was but one addition to a long line of jeremiads on
the subject.

Dirty Hands

The development of the realist brand of public philosophy in the postwar era can be seen as a natural outgrowth of the search for responsible
power. Without a public philosophy—a consensus reflecting the norms
and values of society—the realists would have been hard pressed to
devise a workable standard of responsibility. Fearing this, the realists
clung to the idea of the public philosophy, using it as their moral an-
chor. The public philosophy expressed high ideals and suggested
guidelines for acceptable political behavior. It became a stable point
from which the realists could pass judgment on political action and
recommend alternatives.

The development of the public philosophy in America continues to
this day under many different names and in many different guises.[29]
Every generation develops its own version in accordance with its own
needs. Not all incarnations of the public philosophy have been based
strictly on natural law, as Lippmann would have had it, but most have
relied on a synthesis similar to the one Lippmann described. Judeo-
Christian ethics, classical philosophy, and modern philosophy and psychology all have figured heavily in most of these incarnations.

All public philosophies, whether they reflect the realist perspective
or not, reveal a general code of morality. All provide a framework in
which to view moral claims, and all suggest a general way of ordering
such claims. The realists made use of these characteristics, capitalizing
on the flexibility that the public philosophy gave them. It allowed them
to express their most idealistic aspirations and simultaneously provided
them with the foundation for solving practical, and often morally
wrenching, political problems. With the public philosophy to stand on,
the realists could afford to aim high, to seek ideal and just solutions to

29. See, for example, James Sellers, *Public Ethics* (New York, 1970), and William
Sullivan, *Reconstructing Public Philosophy* (Berkeley, 1982).

political problems. On the other hand, when such solutions proved impossible to achieve, the public philosophy allowed its adherents—in fact it *compelled* them—to opt for the best possible practical solution, even if that solution fell short of the ideal.

Holding themselves accountable to the standards set by the public philosophy, the realists were anything but advocates of amoral power politics; however, they understood that sometimes the responsible (and hence the moral) thing to do was to engage in less-than-virtuous activity—provided, of course, that it was done in the pursuit of a higher ideal. This understanding was in keeping with the realist belief that the political world, by definition, was fraught with immorality, and that the exercise of responsible power was, at times, the choosing of the lesser of two evils. The realists were perceptive enough to know that the term *responsible power*, if not an outright oxymoron, at least implied something of a paradox. They understood that responsible power was a messy concept, and that anyone involved with it was likely to emerge with dirty hands.

In acknowledging that it was virtually impossible for a responsible political actor to emerge from the political world morally unscathed, the realists obviously were very much aware that responsible action is not always congruent with the most innocent and purest action. As Weber warned, politics is no place for a person intent on saving his virtue. The truly responsible political actor, as Niebuhr might have phrased it, is the person who is willing to take "morally hazardous actions" to preserve higher ideals.[30]

Aware of man's inability to live solely within Lippmann's realm of essence, where all is pure, the wielder of responsible power is willing to act in the realm of existence, losing his innocence in the pursuit of a noble cause. His obligation does not end there, however, for in engaging in such questionable activity he assumes some measure of guilt. In order to cleanse himself of the burden of this guilt, he must acknowledge his actions to those whom he serves.

Thus the wielder of responsible power is the most moral political

30. See Reinhold Niebuhr, *The Irony of American History* (New York, 1952), 5.

62

actor of all: he is truly a statesman. He is ardently faithful to the highest of ideals, yet he is not deluded into thinking that he can operate exclusively within the idealistic realm of essence. As someone with consequentialist tendencies, he is most concerned that the *result* of his action be in keeping with the moral code established by the public philosophy and be in the best interests of his constituents. As a representative of the people, the statesman understands that he acts as an agent for them: he is responsible for their safety and well-being. If his duties as protector of his constituents take him into morally hazardous ground, he must forge ahead in spite of the qualms he may have. As a forthright statesman, however, he is unafraid to reveal what he has done. By showing his dirty hands, he in effect shows his credentials as a wielder of responsible power.

The political philosopher Michael Walzer summarized these points as follows: "Here is the moral politician: it is by his dirty hands that we know him. If he were a moral man and nothing else, his hands would not be dirty; if he were a politician and nothing else, he would pretend that they were clean." [31] For Walzer and the realists, the moral man who is incapable of dirtying his hands is as poor a political actor as the politician who has dirty hands but pretends they are clean. The true moral man and statesman—the wielder of responsible power—is willing to dirty his hands and admit to the world that they are dirty. To have dirty hands is to suffer, and there is no glory in it, but such is the nature of political action.

The statesman works his way through his dilemmas by using the Weberian scheme that takes into account the ethics of "ultimate ends" and "responsibility." He evaluates his behavior in terms of the moral continuum, weighing his personal conscience, his duties as a statesman, and the circumstances with which he is confronted. In holding himself responsible, he inevitably must be guided by the moral standards—and the public philosophy—of the people he represents. The decision to pursue a morally hazardous action in defense of a noble

31. Michael Walzer, "Political Action: The Problem of Dirty Hands," *Philosophy and Public Affairs*, II (Winter, 1973), 168.

cause is among the most wrenching that a statesman must make. Yet generally, the people whom the statesman represents give indications as to what they perceive to be justifiable and what they deem to be immoral.

The notion of "dirty hands" in itself may be distasteful, especially as it lends credence to charges of maintaining a dual standard of morality—which the realists in fact fought against. But when the dirty-hands concept is balanced with the countervailing values that it serves, it becomes quite useful. For example, a statesman defending prudence cannot act out of passion, anger, or revenge; in defending humility he cannot act out of self-righteousness; in defending the careful consideration of ideals as against self-interests he cannot be driven by narrow cost-benefit analyses; in defending democracy he cannot act as a dictator. In short, responsible power allows for dirty hands so long as the dirt is not picked up too far from the values the hands were meant to protect.

The realists criticized the people and government of the United States for not facing up to the fact that like all political actors, the United States as a nation has dirty hands: like the politician who denies the fact that his hands are dirty, the American people and many of their leaders preferred to overlook that aspect of their political life, thinking of themselves, instead, as the moral man who would never dirty his hands in the first place. The realists argued that not only were the people and politicians of the United States deluding themselves, but even if their image of the nation was accurate, the United States then could not be exercising responsible power. No nation can be responsible without engaging in some morally ambiguous acts and admitting that in some cases it acts with dirty hands. Events in the world are not so harmonious that ideals and self-interest will never clash. Thus, in terms of the dirty-hands concept, the realists had two complaints: first, that the people and politicians in the United States were harboring illusions about their nation's ability to maintain its innocence in international affairs; second, that these same people mistook responsibility for a static ideal rather than an evolving guideline for political action.

64

"The irony of our situation," Niebuhr wrote in 1954, "lies in the fact that we could not be virtuous (in the sense of practicing the virtues which are implicit in meeting our vast world responsibilities) if we are really as innocent as we pretend to be." If we were so innocent, he argued, we would not be fulfilling the dictates of responsible power: we would not be making the hard choices that responsible power demands of us. On the other hand, Niebuhr called attention to the fact that "our dreams of pure virtue are dissolved in a situation in which it is possible to exercise the virtue of responsibility toward a community of nations only by courting the prospective guilt of the atomic bomb." [32] With these words, he not only was trying to enlighten his fellow Americans about the realities of responsible power politics and its implications for the nuclear world, but he also was giving voice to the most difficult question of all: What, exactly, does responsible power mean when it comes to the use or threatened use of nuclear weapons?

32. Niebuhr, *Irony of American History*, 23.

3 Usable and Unusable Force

Warsaw and Rotterdam, London and Coventry, Cologne and Nuremberg, Hiroshima and Nagasaki, are stepping stones, not only in the development of the modern technology of war, but also in the development of the modern morality of warfare.

—*Hans Morgenthau, 1948*

War today is no longer the continuation of diplomacy by other means. War now destroys the victor with the vanquished.

—*Hans Morgenthau, 1950*

All too often responsibility remains an unarticulated, visceral feeling. There is no denying that ideas about responsibility frequently are tied to personal, emotional responses to particular or individual circumstances. But such ideas are also the products of larger, historical circumstances. As times change, perceptions of what constitutes responsible behavior inevitably change with them. In fact, as we shall see, responsibility is especially sensitive to historical change. It stands to reason that when a revolution in war fighting occurs—as when machine guns, submarines, poison gas, or nuclear bombs are introduced into battle—concurrent upheavals in moral reasoning, including thinking about the problem of responsibility, naturally follow. The moral quandary presented by the advent of total war was a classic case of such an upheaval. In keeping with their penchant for considerations of this kind, the realists did not allow the idea of responsibility in this context to go unexamined.

The bombing of Pearl Harbor in 1941 all but ended the realists' need to argue with pacifists regarding the use of force. Although Niebuhr continued to spend some time refuting pacifist arguments, even he turned most of his attention to the actual conduct of the war. Using the terminology of Augustine and other theorists of the "just war," Niebuhr and the other realists turned to the problem of *jus in bello* (justice in war) rather than *jus ad bellum* (justice of war). They were no longer interested in *whether* the United States should be fighting. They were now interested in *how* the war should be fought.

Generally speaking, the reasons for fighting were self-evident. Besides self-defense and promoting the cause of freedom around the world, the United States was, as the realists saw it, becoming the principal bulwark against international anarchy. Without American participation in the global war, the establishment of a stable world order would be impossible. As Niebuhr put it: "The world must find a way of avoiding complete anarchy in its international life; and America must find a way to use its great power responsibly. These two needs are organically related; for the world problem cannot be solved if America does not accept its full share of responsibility in solving it." [1] Most Americans agreed with this assessment: isolationism, for the time being, was dead. The problem lay in defining what it meant to use power (and military force) responsibly in wartime.

The Nazi blitzes and Pearl Harbor made it abundantly clear that the nature of military engagement had changed. As a relatively new phenomenon, total war gave rise to a number of unprecedented dilemmas. Chief among those dilemmas was reconciling the old problem of ends and means with the new circumstances. In emphasizing that point, the realists came to rely on the central argument of the nineteenth-century European thinker Karl von Clausewitz.

Clausewitz, author of the magisterial *On War* (1832), was best known for his dictum, "War is the continuation of politics by other means." Implicit in that statement was that war should be waged for the achievement of political goals; in other words, war, properly con-

---

1. Reinhold Niebuhr, "American Power and World Responsibility," *Christianity and Crisis*, III (April 5, 1943), 2.

ceived, should be merely a means by which a nation attempts to achieve a political end. Like any other tool at the statesman's disposal, it should be an instrument of policy and nothing more. Clausewitz advised that in contemplating war the most critical question should be, "De quoi s'agit-il?" ("What is it all about?"). In his opinion, the use of force was desirable only in order to move a nation closer to specific political objectives, and it could be considered successful or unsuccessful only to the extent that it accomplished or failed to accomplish this.[2]

Niebuhr saw the use of force in much the same way. His early debates with pacifists prepared him well to deal with this issue. In 1932, in *Moral Man and Immoral Society*, he suggested that the use of force could be justified provided that it be precisely directed and quickly ended. He wrote that "if violence can be justified at all, its terror must have the tempo of a surgeon's skill and healing must follow quickly upon its wounds."[3] The use of force had to be finely calibrated; it could be used only selectively and for the purpose of achieving realistic, tangible, and immediately attainable results. Niebuhr summarily condemned uses of force that could be construed as random. Randomness was a sure sign of the disconnection of ends and means; for Niebuhr, it was also a sure sign of unusable force. Although Niebuhr put forth these opinions in reference to the use of force in class conflict, he later extrapolated them to conflict between nations. Throughout the 1940s and beyond, this continued to be Niebuhr's position on the use of force in international affairs.

Niebuhr's surgical analogy was not without its problems, particularly in light of the development of modern warfare. Calibrating ends and means was almost impossible in conflicts where discernible boundaries had vanished. In World War II, the old battle fronts where trenches marked the parameters of conflict were gone; the new battle-

2. See Karl von Clausewitz, *On War* (1832; rpr. Princeton, N.J., 1976). For two thought-provoking adaptations of Clausewitz to the nuclear age, see Bernard Brodie, *War and Politics* (New York, 1973), and Sissela Bok, *A Strategy for Peace: Human Values and the Threat of War* (New York, 1989).

3. Reinhold Niebuhr, *Moral Man and Immoral Society: A Study in Ethics and Politics* (New York, 1932), 220.

field was limited only by the range of the combatants' bombers. How could force be directed with surgical precision when everyone, in one way or another, was a participant in the war, when the line between military and civilian was becoming increasingly obscure, and when "war efforts" encompassed virtually all activity within the warring nations? And how was Niebuhr's suggestion that "healing must follow quickly" to be implemented when nations were fighting ruthless battles in pursuit of "unconditional surrender"?

These issues were among the thorniest that faced those who thought about the problems of *jus in bello* and total war. Morgenthau later wrote that "the wars of the twentieth century have become everybody's business in the sense not only of nationalistic identification but also of military or economic participation." War, he continued, "has become total not only in the sense of everybody being a prospective participant in war but also in the sense of everybody being a prospective victim in warfare." [4] War in the twentieth century meant "total war waged by total populations for total stakes." [5] Under such conditions, what could *jus in bello* and a reasonable consideration of ends and means possibly mean?

Morgenthau and Kennan ruefully observed that technology was an inextricable part of the problem. Modern mechanized warfare was undergoing a technological revolution that would reach a climax with the creation of the atomic bomb. In the era of mechanized *total* war, the political and economic structures of a nation at war would make it impossible to distinguish the combatant from the noncombatant, the legitimate target from the innocent bystander. In which category, for example, would the university-based rocket scientist fall? What of the civilian factory worker who assembled weaponry, the truck driver who transported it, or the technician who maintained it? Was any one of these cogs in the new war machine any more or less a combatant than the military pilot who dropped a bomb from an airplane or the serviceman who pushed a button to launch a missile?

4. Hans Morgenthau, *Politics Among Nations: The Struggle For Power and Peace* (6th ed., New York, 1985), 397–98.
5. *Ibid.*, 412.

Morgenthau and Kennan despaired over questions such as these, but they also began to wonder whether the questions even mattered. It became clear to them that they faced a cruel irony: even if they could come to some understanding as to what distinguished a combatant from a noncombatant, the new weapons of mass destruction could not be used in such a way as to maintain that distinction. By their very nature, weapons of mass destruction were indiscriminate: they were so large and cumbersome that it was impossible to use them in a limited fashion, let alone with a surgeon's skill.[6]

Kennan was at his most eloquent in denouncing weapons of mass destruction, and he was the most instructive of the realists in defining the idea of usable and unusable force. After almost a decade of arguing against the atomic bomb's further development, he called the bomb "a sterile and hopeless weapon which may for a time serve as an answer of sorts to itself as an uncertain shield against cataclysm, but which cannot in any way serve the purposes of a constructive and hopeful foreign policy." According to Kennan, echoing Clausewitz: "The true end of political action is, after all, to affect the deeper convictions of men; this the atomic bomb cannot do. The suicidal nature of this weapon renders it unsuitable both as a sanction of diplomacy and as the basis of an alliance. Such a weapon is simply not one with which one can usefully support political desiderata; nor is it one with which one readily springs to the defense of one's friends. There can be no coherent relations between such a weapon and the normal objects of national policy."[7] In Kennan's view, the problem with all weapons of mass destruction, especially atomic weapons, was that they failed the ends-and-means test utterly. There was no way to *use* the weapon ef-

6. Later, when the weapons were scaled down and made more accurate in the form of tactical nuclear weapons, the realists' fear shifted to the problem of escalation. Even if the weapons were more precise, they were still relatively uncontrollable, and they were destabilizing from the standpoint of maintaining the "balance of power." Who could say where the nuclear exchanges of these smaller weapons would end, especially when they were being used in the field alongside conventional weaponry?

7. George Kennan, *The Nuclear Delusion: Soviet-American Relations in the Atomic Age* (New York, 1982), 7.

fectively to achieve a political objective. Once a nation resorted to indiscriminate force, it ceased to have a favorable chance of achieving its political objectives.

In 1966, in a letter to Louis Halle, Kennan elaborated on his ideas about weapons of mass destruction, nuclear or otherwise. He maintained that such weapons have no rational political application and that American reliance on them was a mistake. He wrote that "weapons of mass destruction, as we are now beginning to see in a very small way in Vietnam, are simply not a rational weapon for the exertion of power and influence internationally where the task of power is to affect the behavior of people and governments, not destroy them."[8] Kennan, like Morgenthau, argued that firepower did not necessarily equal political power, that bombs did not always translate into control, and that conventional mass bombings like those taking place in Vietnam were doomed to failure.

From the outset, Kennan and the other realists were skeptical of the terms *victory* and *defeat*, especially where the use of weapons of mass destruction was concerned. They simply did not believe that a nuclear war could be "won" in any meaningful sense. Nuclear war against the Soviet Union would mean retaliation and devastation, and the use of nuclear weapons against lesser powers would mean military victory but not necessarily a favorable political settlement. Besides their function as a deterrent, Kennan saw only one possible use for nuclear weapons: as instruments of compulsion through the making of offensive threats. But he adamantly opposed any such use of them. As he put it, he "tended to agree with Stalin's view" that threatening to use atomic weapons was something you did "if you liked to threaten people with weak nerves."[9] He did not believe that nations with nuclear capability were likely to follow through on their nuclear threats. The stakes were too high, the line between victory and defeat too muddled.

This reasoning pointed to an all-important confluence between practical and moral considerations. As Kennan and the other realists

8. George Kennan to Louis Halle, April 20, 1966, in Box 31, George F. Kennan Papers, Princeton University, Princeton, N.J.

9. George Kennan to Gar Alperovitz, January 11, 1965, in Box 31, Kennan Papers.

conceived of it, usable force was force that met at least minimum practical and moral requirements. Conversely, unusable force was force that by its very nature was both impractical and immoral—impractical because of the disjunction between the stated ends and the means used to achieve them, and therefore immoral. This confluence, to be sure, was no accident. Usable force was considered moral *because* it held the promise of accountability.

As thinkers concerned with accountability—a practical matter with moral connotations—the realists favored only those uses of force that sought to balance ends and means. In an age of increasing automation and mechanization, an era in which individuals seemed to be losing control over their inventions, the realists took a stand against the inexorable march of technology. Despite the reality of total war, they argued for a traditional conception of responsibility and accountability: standards had to be upheld. Although the uncertainties of total war inevitably would blur some features of the moral landscape, the realists kept their focus on maintaining strict accountability.

Beginning with their commentaries on area, or "obliteration," bombing of civilian targets during World War II, the realists attempted to show that even in total war, policy makers had to be attentive to the practical and moral necessity of correlating ends and means when deciding on the use of force. Niebuhr put it concisely: "We do not claim that it is easy to draw a line between what is permissible and what is not in a 'total' war. We recognize that a technical society has increased the totalitarian character of war. We believe nevertheless that lines can be drawn and that a line against 'obliteration' bombing is possible." [10] This claim became increasingly relevant and central to realist thinking when considered in connection with the ultimate in area bombings— the firebombings of cities such as Dresden and Tokyo, and the atomic bombings of Hiroshima and Nagasaki. It also figured conspicuously in the discussions leading to the decision to build a still more awesome weapon of mass destruction, the hydrogen bomb.

10. Reinhold Niebuhr, "Editorial Notes," *Christianity and Crisis*, IV (April 17, 1944), 2.

From Area Bombing to Building the H-Bomb

By the middle of 1943, when the Nazi blitzes of London, Coventry, and other cities were answered by Allied raids on Hamburg, Dusseldorf, and other urban centers deep in the heart of Germany, each side had experienced total war from both the attacking and receiving ends. Total war had become a reality primarily in the form of area bombing. What distinguished this kind of attack from most previous military bombardments was that the raids were directed at civilian rather than military targets. (*Directed*, however, only loosely describes these raids since, by design, the bombs fell unpredictably.) Strategically, the chief purpose of area bombing was twofold: to disrupt the civilian economy of the enemy, thereby draining his war effort of much-needed support; and to destroy the morale of the average citizen, perhaps weakening domestic political support for the war.

From the outset, the realists were skeptical. Area bombing was entirely different from the accepted tactic of "precision" bombing, and the realists were quick to make this distinction. Precision bombings were "directed" in a much narrower sense of the word: they were launched at specific targets, usually military or industrial installations. The idea behind precision bombing was to destroy targets of vital strategic importance to the enemy's war effort—for example, V-1 and V-2 rocket sites, oil storage installations, and armament factories. The idea behind area bombing was to saturate a densely populated area with bombs for the purpose of destroying large chunks of civilian habitat rather than any specific strategic target.[11]

Allied area raids generally were conducted at night and usually consisted in the dropping of high explosives, incendiaries, and fragmentation bombs. On occasion, when local conditions were of a certain configuration, firestorms resulted. In Hamburg, Kassel, Darmstadt, Dresden, and Tokyo firestorms broke out after concentrated incendiary attacks on those heavily built-up areas. The damage inflicted was enormous. In Hamburg, for example, the bombings of July and Au-

11. See U.S. Strategic Bombing Survey, *Overall Report: European War* (Washington, D.C., 1945), 70–72.

gust, 1943, resulted in physical damage to between 55 and 60 percent of the city. Of the 30 square miles damaged, 12.5 were completely burned out. At least 60,000 people were killed (a conservative estimate, according to the United States Strategic Bombing Survey) and 750,000 were left homeless after one-third of all dwellings in the city were destroyed. Many of the victims died of carbon monoxide poisoning, suffocating in the bomb shelters where they sought refuge.[12]

Ever since its inception the practice of area bombing has been hotly debated. One important question is whether such pummeling does in fact demoralize its victims. Other questions concern the efficiency and effectiveness of the method. Finally, of course, an enduring issue has been the moral one.[13] Many observers have speculated on whether area bombing can be considered a just use of force and a responsible use of power. The realists' reservations about the practice focused on the ends-and-means problem. Their qualms were similar to but even more pointed than those first expressed in the Strategic Bombing Survey.

This survey, commissioned by President Roosevelt and Secretary of War Henry Stimson in 1944 and completed in 1946, was the first government effort to examine systematically the effects of Allied destruction of enemy targets.[14] The team assembled to compile the data and write the reports was an impressive one. Its chairman was Franklin D'Olier, president of Prudential Insurance; among its directors were George Ball, John Kenneth Galbraith, and Paul Nitze. This collection of businessmen, academicians, and government officials reached some surprising conclusions, particularly in regard to the efficacy of area bombing.

One finding was that although area bombing directed against cities

12. *Ibid.*, 74, 92–99.

13. For the best account of the history of strategic bombing and its moral implications, see Ronald Schaffer, *Wings of Judgment: American Bombing in World War II* (New York, 1985).

14. For a comprehensive history of the U.S. Strategic Bombing Survey, see David MacIssac, *Strategic Bombing in World War II: The Story of the United States Strategic Bombing Survey* (New York, 1976). See also Kenneth P. Werell, "The Strategic Bombing of Germany in World War II," *Journal of American History*, LXXIII (December, 1986), 702–13.

did seriously dampen morale, it did not depress and discourage citizens enough to fatally weaken the enemy war effort. The survey's European report of 1945 stated that the bombing of German cities produced the "psychological effects of defeatism, fear, hopelessness, fatalism and apathy" but that, all things considered, this lowering of morale was not a decisive factor in the war. What won the war in Germany, as far as air power was concerned, was the prudent use of air attacks against carefully selected military and industrial targets. Ultimately, the destruction of ball-bearing and rubber-processing plants was more devastating to the German war effort than the area bombings of Hamburg and Dresden.[15]

The survey's conclusions cast a long shadow over the strategy of area bombing. A vast amount of statistical evidence was compiled in the survey, and much of this evidence raised doubts about the bombings' effectiveness: one could conclude from reading the survey that area bombing was a formidable method of intimidation but that it was not a "winning weapon." And even though the survey never really addressed the moral issue directly, its writers did incorporate their moral doubts into their evaluation of the strategy's effectiveness. The realists handled the subject in a similar fashion, and their ruminations were dominated by a similar refrain.

Niebuhr was certainly not alone in his call for the "drawing of lines" concerning area bombing. Lippmann's "The Responsibility of the German Nation" (a "Today and Tomorrow" column appearing in November, 1943) was typical of the realists' ongoing response. Lippmann called attention to the moral aspects of the destruction of German cities and suggested that the destruction should weigh heavily upon the consciences of the Allies: "We should dishonor ourselves and our cause if we did not face with a candid conscience our moral responsibility in the devastation of German cities. For obviously we cannot be satisfied to say that we are now doing what the enemy did first. We reject his standards, and therefore, cannot stoop to justify our actions

15. Strategic Bombing Survey, *European War,* 95–99. See also *ibid.,* "Conclusions," 107–108.

by his standards."[16] Lippmann took no solace in the fact that the Allies were merely fighting fire with fire.

Lippmann did recognize, however, that bombing could not be completely avoided by the Allies in Europe. Like the other realists, he maintained that bombing could be justified so long as it was not merely a haphazard use of violence. His reasoning was simple: if the Allies did not use their power to win the war as quickly as possible, then they were not using that power responsibly. Every day that the war continued, countless innocents were killed. So, reasoned Lippmann, "if we refrain from attacking the cities like Berlin, Hamburg, Cologne, from which the subjugation of Europe is directed, implemented and enforced, still more innocent people of all sorts in the captive nations must perish."[17] In short, a case could be made that *not* bombing was unacceptable.

As the war went on, Lippmann continued to justify Allied bombings directed at the German war machine. At one point he wrote that the war in the air was justified as long as the Allies were "systematically attacking and seeking to destroy the German airforce." He concluded: "The ultimate purpose of all these military operations is not to kill our enemies or to terrorize them or to make them suffer. It is to render them harmless by knocking some arms out of their hands in order to compel them to lay down the rest of their arms."[18] For Lippmann, what justified a raid was the idea that it was not a terror raid but a military operation. He did not complain very much, however, when the Allies exceeded this limitation.

Niebuhr was much more vocal on this point. In "Is the Bombing Necessary?" (appearing in April, 1944), Niebuhr argued that area bombing was so qualitatively different from precision bombing that the Allied command owed the people an explanation for using such a tac-

16. Walter Lippmann, "The Responsibility of the German Nation" ("Today and Tomorrow," November 27, 1943), in Walter Lippmann Papers, Yale University, New Haven.

17. *Ibid.*

18. Walter Lippmann, "The War in the Air" ("Today and Tomorrow," March 11, 1944), in Lippmann Papers.

tic. In Niebuhr's opinion, the change from precision to area bombing was too significant to remain unexamined. He wondered why "the government has never thought it necessary to explain or justify this change of strategy," adding, "Do we not have the right to know what prompted this change?" [19]

With this article Niebuhr revealed his basic distrust of the "military mind." Such a mentality, he observed, "is inclined to disregard moral and political factors in strategy and it is therefore unsafe to give it a final moral and political authority in matters of this kind." As a corrective to the dominance of the military in making decisions on basic strategy, Niebuhr proposed the notion of democratic review. He conceded that "laymen are not capable of judging detailed problems of strategy," but he argued that nevertheless, "*general principles* of strategy ought to remain under democratic scrutiny." [20] This was Niebuhr's version of the old adage that war is too important to be left to the generals.

Niebuhr's characteristic vigilance on behalf of democratic principles permeated "Is the Bombing Necessary?" The point of the piece was to instruct his readers to ask questions about the policies that were being pursued in their name. The most pertinent question, as far as he was concerned, regarded the justification of area bombing. He urged his readers to ask themselves whether they thought it justified, and not to take the position of the Allied command as the final word on the matter.

For his part, Niebuhr had grave reservations about area bombing. He seemed to be willing to accept it only as a last resort, and even then somewhat grudgingly. Area bombing could be just, in Niebuhr's view, only in the direst of circumstances—circumstances that did not seem to him to exist in 1944. He was not wholly convinced that area bombing was necessary to win the war (at least in Europe). In any event, he was not willing to let the military and government establishments go unchallenged on their assumption that it *was* necessary. The strategy of area bombing—of dubious moral quality to begin with—also was

19. Reinhold Niebuhr, "Is the Bombing Necessary?" *Christianity and Crisis*, IV (April 3, 1944), 1.
20. *Ibid.* Emphasis mine.

proving to be ineffective. Niebuhr noted that German morale had actually improved in some places in spite of the Allied bombardments—a point that later was substantiated in the Strategic Bombing Survey. The moral issue, combined with the question of effectiveness, left Niebuhr extremely skeptical, although while the fighting continued he did not go so far as to denounce area bombing as being patently unacceptable.

"The bombing of cities," Niebuhr wrote, "is a vivid revelation of the moral ambiguity of warfare." He took it to be an unfortunate and inescapable fact of life that "once bombing has been developed as an instrument of warfare, it is not possible to disavow its use without capitulating to the foe who refuses to disavow it."[21] Niebuhr firmly believed that as long as nations had bombs and were willing to use them on cities, the Allies had no choice but to be willing and able to do the same. He believed just as deeply, however, that this situation did not absolve the Allies from using this weaponry judiciously.

It was one thing to justify the use of weapons of mass destruction with some stipulations attached; it was quite another to give governmental and military planners free rein. Niebuhr was treading a fine line: he wanted to limit something that was exceedingly difficult to limit; he wanted tight control over weapons that did not lend themselves to control. At the very least, he succeeded in calling attention to the restrictions that needed to be considered in relation to the use of massive force. This was no small accomplishment considering the wartime milieu.

That milieu, although not one of hysteria, was one of more-than-mild agitation. With the home front mobilized and the war effort proceeding vigorously, constraints on bombing tactics were not the first thing most people considered. The pursuit of unconditional surrender with the express goal of liberating oppressed peoples from the shackles of totalitarianism did not lend itself to constraint; neither did the idea that American casualties would mount to staggering levels should an invasion of the Japanese main islands become necessary. This was the

21. Reinhold Niebuhr, "The Bombing of Germany," *Christianity and Society*, VIII (Summer, 1943), 3–4.

context in which the immediate responses to the escalation of area bombing were formed.

When area bombing gave way to atomic bombing in 1945, the arguments remained the same. The connection between area and atomic attacks was unmistakable. Niebuhr called the use of the atomic bomb "merely the culmination of our strategy of total war involving the use of ever more powerful obliteration bombing and incendiarism." Area bombing had created a moral climate in which atomic bombing was thinkable; it was but a short leap from the firebombings of Dresden and Tokyo to the atomic bombings of Hiroshima and Nagasaki. This fact gave little comfort to Niebuhr, who wrote: "The thoughtful element in the democratic world has a very uneasy conscience about the use of the bomb against the Japanese. Critics have rightly pointed out that we reached the level of Nazi morality in justifying the use of the bomb on the grounds that it shortened the war. That is exactly what the Nazis said about the destruction of Rotterdam and Warsaw." [22] Niebuhr liked to think of himself as belonging in the camp of the "thoughtful element" with the "very uneasy conscience." Although he could justify the use of the bomb as an evil that had to be done in order to do good, he could not overlook the guilt that accompanied it.

Niebuhr's confusion was reflected in the contradictory positions he took after the Japanese surrender. Initially he signed a statement issued by a special commission of the Federal Council of Churches that condemned the "surprise bombings of Hiroshima and Nagasaki" as "morally indefensible." Soon afterward he reneged on that statement, suggesting in an editorial in *Christianity and Society* that the statesmen who made decisions on the development and use of the atomic bomb were virtually duty-bound to act as they did. "It is a simple matter to condemn the statesmen," he wrote. "The question is whether they were not driven by historic forces more powerful than any human decision." [23]

22. Reinhold Niebuhr, "The Atomic Bomb," *Christianity and Society*, X (Fall, 1945), 4.

23. Reinhold Niebuhr, *Love and Justice: Selections from the Shorter Writings of Reinhold Niebuhr* (Philadelphia, 1957), 232–33. For more on Niebuhr's vacillation on this issue see Richard Fox, *Reinhold Niebuhr: A Biography* (New York, 1985), 224–25.

After his initial wavering, Niebuhr stuck with his conclusion that the bombings of Hiroshima and Nagasaki were morally defensible but that they brought with them a heavy burden. The bombings were defensible because they were a rational means for achieving a specific policy objective—winning the war. The correlation between ends and means was clear and calculable, and there was little doubt that this last use of force would result in peace. There would be no reprisals and no threat of all-out nuclear war, since the United States had the only atomic bombs in existence. There would be merely an end to hostilities.[24] Niebuhr did criticize the use of the bomb as showing a "lack of imagination." He was impressed by the idea of a demonstration, such as the one discussed by the Interim Committee, President Truman's advisory board on atomic weapons. He thought that such a demonstration might have been an effective means of impressing upon the Japanese people that the war was over. Perhaps a demonstration would have eliminated the need to use the bomb on Japanese cities; at the very least, it might have eased the moral burden should the United States have been left with no alternative but to use the weapon on densely populated areas. In either case, Niebuhr thought this option had considerable merit.

Lippmann had no such equivocal response to the atomic bombings, at least none that he cared to share with the public. The bombs dropped while he was vacationing at his usual summer retreat in Maine, and the entire episode escaped immediate commentary in his regular column. By the time he returned to Washington and began writing again, the story was old news.[25] As the final salvo of World War II, the use of atomic weapons did not seem to trouble Lippmann much. As a weapon for future conflicts, however, the atomic bomb worried him deeply.

24. See Reinhold Niebuhr and Hans Morgenthau, "The Ethics of War and Peace in the Nuclear Age," *War/Peace Report*, VII (February, 1967), 3–8. See also Morgenthau's evaluation of Niebuhr's response to atomic weaponry in Harold Landon, ed., *Reinhold Niebuhr: A Prophetic Voice in Our Time* (Greenwich, Conn., 1962), esp. 107.

25. See Ronald Steel, *Walter Lippmann and the American Century* (Boston, 1980), 424–25.

Most people were intrigued with the awesome power of the new weapon; Lippmann was intrigued with its limits. The discovery and use of atomic weapons did not fill him with optimism about its possible effects on American foreign policy in the postwar world; on the contrary, it made him wary. "There is no more difficult art than to exercise great power well," he wrote. "All the serious military, diplomatic, and economic decisions we have now to take will depend on how correctly we measure our power, how truly we see its possibilities *within* its limitations." [26] Just because this newly found power was harnessed and used successfully to end the war did not mean that it would be equally useful in the future.

Not until after the Bikini atoll bomb tests of 1946 did Lippmann fully discuss atomic power in terms of usable and unusable force. He hinted at the problem in late 1945 and early 1946 in his frequent commentaries on arms control, but he did not offer a decisive opinion on it until nearly a year after Hiroshima and Nagasaki. "We must be careful not to overestimate the military value of the atomic bomb," he wrote. "It would, for example, be unusable, even as a threat, at Trieste and Venezia Giula. Almost certainly it would be worse than useless. For the bomb would be useless against Tito's infantry since it would kill our own troops as well as his, and if he overran Trieste, could we kill all the Italians we are trying to defend in that city in order to expel Tito's troops from that city?" [27] Would the United States really detonate atomic bombs over Vienna, Rome, Copenhagen, or Paris to defend those cities? What sort of defense would it be that resulted in annihilation? Again, the problem boiled down to the fact that atomic weapons were indiscriminate instruments of mass destruction. They were, in most situations, literally unusable as a means to attain a rational end.

Acheson saw the potential hazards of the atomic bomb as soon as it was unveiled. For him as for many others, the thrill of victory was accompanied by a wave of dread. On the evening of August 6, 1945, just

26. Walter Lippmann quoted *ibid.*, 425; quotation is taken from "The Rise of the United States" ("Today and Tomorrow," September 11, 1945).

27. Walter Lippmann, "Bikini" ("Today and Tomorrow," June 29, 1946) in Lippmann Papers.

after the destruction of Hiroshima, Acheson wrote: "The news of the atomic bomb is the most frightening yet. If we can't work out some sort of organization of great powers, we shall be gone geese for fair. It makes the prospect of Ed Stettinius as our representative on the U.N. even more fantastic than ever."[28]

Acheson's instincts led him to the immediate conclusion that the most important thing about the atomic bomb was to limit its use. His first thought was that this was a job too important for Stettinius, a man whom Acheson described as having "gone far with comparatively modest equipment."[29] The need for arms control would be paramount, and the best people would be needed to pursue it. Acheson could hardly have objected when, later, he and David Lilienthal, chairman of the Atomic Energy Commission (AEC), were selected by President Truman and Secretary of State James F. Byrnes to draft the first and most important arms-control recommendations of the postwar era. The Acheson-Lilienthal Report became the foundation for the first atomic arms-control proposal ever: the Baruch Plan.

Acheson, like most Americans, never seriously questioned the propriety of using the atomic bomb against Japan. Along with the rest of the realists, however, he could not escape a feeling of gloom. Kennan expressed the prevailing dissatisfaction when he called the bombings an instance of "regrettable extremism born of the bad precedent of the conventional strategic bombings."[30] This opinion would only grow stronger among the realists as time passed; statements like Kennan's made it plain to them that they had stretched their own logic to its extreme.

If they thought they had reached that extreme with Hiroshima and Nagasaki, however, they were wrong. They had more tests coming in the ongoing debate concerning the acceptability of the existence of nuclear weapons and in the growing pressures of the arms race. The de-

28. Dean Acheson, *Present at the Creation: My Years in the State Department* (New York, 1969), 113.

29. *Ibid.*, 88.

30. See Kennan, *Nuclear Delusion,* xiv; see also George Kennan to Eugene Rabinowitch, September 11, 1956, in Kennan Papers.

cision as to whether the United States would pursue an all-out plan to build a hydrogen "superbomb" was only the first such test.

In late 1949 and early 1950, the debate on this issue was intense. On one side, proponents of the H-bomb such as Edward Teller insisted that development of the weapon was essential, especially since the Soviets were threatening to achieve nuclear parity or even superiority. Opponents such as J. Robert Oppenheimer, the man who directed America's first atomic-weapons project, argued that the new weapon would be not only impractical but also an invitation to genocide. The battle between Teller, who became known as "the father of the H-bomb," and Oppenheimer, already known as "the father of the A-bomb," was symbolic of the ambivalence that reigned.[31] Many Americans shuddered at the prospect of weapons vastly more powerful than those used against Japan; at the same time, the same people shuddered at the mere thought that the Soviets were closing the gap.

The dilemmas facing Acheson—the most visible of the realists because of his pivotal role as secretary of state—exemplified the complexities of the issue. As the controversy heated up in late 1949, Truman appointed a special three-man committee to deal with the problem. Its members were Acheson, AEC chairman Lilienthal, and the secretary of defense, Louis Johnson. This committee was instructed to study the question of whether to proceed with the project and then make a recommendation to the president. Johnson, it was known, was strongly in favor of the weapon; Lilienthal was just as adamantly opposed. Everyone, including Truman, knew that Acheson would cast the deciding vote.[32]

Acheson sought advice from the usual sources, which at that time included the outgoing director of the Policy Planning staff, George Kennan, and Kennan's deputy and soon-to-be replacement, Paul Nitze. As happened to others who solicited Kennan's opinions at vari-

31. For a summary of the scientists' activities, see Alice K. Smith, *A Peril and a Hope* (Chicago, 1965), and Fred Kaplan, *The Wizards of Armageddon* (New York, 1983). For an example of their writing, see J. Robert Oppenheimer, *The Open Mind* (New York, 1955).

32. For the story of this special committee, see Barton Bernstein, "Truman and the H-Bomb," *Bulletin of the Atomic Scientists*, XL (March, 1984), 12–18.

ous times over his career, Acheson got more than he bargained for. The result was no minor memorandum but a sweeping, sometimes lyrical *tour de force* filling more than seventy pages. Kennan emptied his soul, and in the course of doing so, produced a document that outlined the views on nuclear weapons that he would hold for decades to come.

Kennan felt that nuclear weapons could not be integrated into the fighting force and that international control had to be achieved. Such control obviously could be attained only as part of an overall settlement with the Soviets concerning, among other things, the German question and the security of Western Europe. Barring a settlement, the United States had to decide how best to defend its interests. Kennan felt strongly that the answer was *not* with nuclear weapons. Instead of Kennan's views on only the specific controversy over the H-bomb, what Acheson got was a primer on politics and war fighting in the nuclear age.

Kennan thought that before deciding on the desirability of building the H-bomb, the administration needed to decide what role the bomb would play within the armed forces. Was it to be an "integral and vitally important component of our military strength, which we would expect to employ deliberately, immediately, and unhesitatingly in the event we become involved in a military conflict with the Soviet Union?" "Or," he asked, "are we to retain such weapons in our national arsenal only as a deterrent to the use of similar weapons against ourselves and our allies as a possible means of retaliation in case they are used?" The problem could be reduced to a single question: "For what purpose . . . are we to develop such weapons and to train our forces in their use?" [33] With these questions, Kennan sounded much like Clausewitz: "De quoi s'agit-il?"

The answer to this fundamental question would determine the answers to all the questions that followed. "If we decide to hold weapons of mass destruction only for deterrent-retaliatory purposes," Kennan wrote, "then the limit on the number and power of the weapons we

33. Kennan, *Nuclear Delusion*, 4; see also Kennan's memo, reprinted in U.S. Department of State, *Foreign Relations of the United States, 1950* (7 vols.; Washington, D.C., 1977), I, 22–44.

should hold is governed by our estimate as to what it would take to make an attack on this country or its allies by weapons of mass destruction a risky, probably unprofitable, and therefore irrational undertaking for any adversary." In that case, the problem of the H-bomb would be easily solvable: build and deploy only as many of them as were necessary to insure deterrence and retaliatory capability. If, however, nuclear weapons were to have any role beyond this—say, as an integral part of the fighting force—then one would have to presume that their purpose would be "to inflict maximum destruction on the forces, population, and territory of the enemy, with the least expenditure of effort, in full acceptance of the attendant risk of retaliation against us." In that case, wrote Kennan, "the only limitations on the number and power of mass destruction weapons which we would wish to develop would presumably be those of ordinary military economy, such as cost, efficiency, and ease of delivery." [34]

Kennan argued strenuously that the best course of action was to keep nuclear weapons for deterrence alone, retaining only as many as were necessary to that purpose. The most important thing was to avoid reliance on nuclear weapons in the course of regular military planning; such weapons should be relegated to the background. This last point meant that the distinction between nuclear and conventional weapons was worth observing. It was an imperfect distinction, to be sure, but, as Kennan wrote, "if we were to reject all distinctions in life on the basis of inexactness and imperfection, no civilization would be possible." In order to save this particular civilization, this particular imprecise distinction would have to be preserved.

Kennan warned his colleagues not to "fall into the error of initiating, or planning to initiate, the employment of these weapons and concepts, thus hypnotizing ourselves into the belief that they may ultimately serve some positive national purpose." [35] He still believed in the possibility of international control, or at least a comprehensive settlement of postwar disputes, and he feared that the H-bomb would scut-

34. Kennan, *Nuclear Delusion*, 5.
35. Department of State, *Foreign Relations of the United States, 1950*, I, 39.

tle any remaining hopes for agreement. He knew that arms control would be impossible if the United States began to depend on nuclear weapons as the backbone of its military force, and he feared that if policy makers listened to those who were advocating the nuclearization of the nation's defenses, there would be little chance of stopping the arms race.

Kennan's fears were well founded. There were those in Washington who thought nuclear weapons had more than deterrent value, and unlike Kennan, they were willing to consider them as usable force. Chief among these people was Paul Nitze, whose influence in the State Department was growing just as Kennan's was diminishing. In the end, Acheson heeded Nitze's advice over Kennan's.

Nitze's view of weapons of mass destruction was diametrically opposite to that of Kennan.[36] He seemed to be able to look at the tragedy of both conventional and atomic bombing more analytically than the temperamental Kennan. Whereas Kennan had been stunned when viewing the rubble left by Allied bombing in Hamburg, Nitze had reacted calmly to the ruins he inspected in Germany and Japan as a member of the Strategic Bombing Survey. Kennan's first thought was that the tragedy of area bombing must never be allowed to happen again. Nitze's response was matter of fact: he concentrated on figuring out what lessons could be learned from the bombings, in case such tactics should be needed in the future.

Nitze's postwar experience, which included tours of Hiroshima and Nagasaki shortly after the bombings, led him to believe that contrary to popular opinion, atomic bombs were not the "absolute weapons" that Bernard Brodie and others made them out to be. In the Strategic Bombing Survey's report, Nitze pointed out that apart from the fallout, the atomic destruction of Hiroshima and Nagasaki was no different from the conventional destruction of cities that were area-bombed. His report estimated that 220 B-29s using incendiary bombs and other high explosives could have inflicted the same damage as the single

36. For an excellent summary of the differences between Kennan and Nitze, as well as a discussion of their personal backgrounds and relationship, see Gregg Herken, "The Great Foreign Policy Fight," *American Heritage*, XXXVII (April–May, 1986), 65–80.

atomic bomb did on Hiroshima, and that 125 B-29s similarly equipped could have caused as much damage as the second bomb did in Nagasaki.[37] This language suggested not only a quantitative equivalence, but also a moral equivalence between the conventional and atomic attacks carried out in the latter stages of the war. The report noted that although the destruction was brutal, it did not completely destroy the cities, and many of those who were shielded from the blasts managed to survive.

The tone of the report reflected Nitze's belief that atomic weapons really were not so totally different from other weapons of mass destruction; they were here to stay and there was a reasonable chance that they might be used again. The key questions in regard to the new weapons, Nitze thought, were how they would be used in the future and with what results. His thoughts turned naturally to bomb shelters, plans for the evacuation of cities, and other moves related to civil defense.[38]

Nitze's position on the H-bomb was in keeping with his general view of U.S.–Soviet relations, a view that gained full expression in 1950 in a National Security Council (NSC) document known as NSC-68. This document, drawn up under Nitze's direction and approved by Truman, Acheson, and the rest of the NSC, called for a build-up of both conventional and nuclear weapons as part of an overall effort to contain communism. The document's recommendations on nuclear weapons were based on the assumption that in a military conflict, both the United States and the Soviet Union would at least have to consider using such weapons. Given this assumption, the United States could not afford to let the Soviets gain the upper hand in this area; therefore, the continued stockpiling of atomic weapons and further research and development of the H-bomb were essential.[39]

37. See U.S. Strategic Bombing Survey, *Summary Report: Pacific War* (Washington, D.C., 1946), 22–25.

38. For a more complete discussion of the evolution of Nitze's views on nuclear weapons, see Alan Tonelson, "Nitze's World," *Foreign Policy,* XXXV (Summer, 1979), 74–90.

39. NSC-68, reprinted in Department of State, *Foreign Relations of the United States, 1950,* I, 234–313.

Over the Christmas weekend in 1949, Acheson went home to ponder the question of whether to endorse the H-bomb project. He had two arguments to consider. On one side he had Kennan (whose views he well knew even though he would not receive Kennan's lengthy memo until mid-January), along with Oppenheimer and Lilienthal. These three believed that the H-bomb was a morally reprehensible instrument of doom, destined to fuel the arms race and kill any hopes for arms control. On the other side Acheson had Nitze, Johnson, and Teller arguing that if the United States did not pursue this weapon, it risked losing its military superiority over the Soviets. All things considered, however, Acheson really did not have much of a decision to make. The political atmosphere was such that he was left with little choice: the Soviet Union was perceived to be an aggressive foe, communism seemed to be on the march, and America's influence around the world seemed to be waning. Public, congressional, and bureaucratic pressure all were forcing Acheson's hand. To forestall the bomb's development would have raised a great furor. Some might even have accused the administration of not protecting the vital interests of the United States and therefore not acting responsibly.

R. Gordon Arneson, a State Department official who assisted Acheson in this matter, suggested that Acheson's "sense of realism prompted him to conclude that even if the Soviet Union refrained from undertaking a thermonuclear program as the result of our refraining— a nonexistent prospect—the Administration would run into a Congressional buzz saw and the proposal would be stillborn." Arneson believed that Acheson was sympathetic to the arguments of Kennan, Oppenheimer, and Lilienthal but was unable to translate these arguments into a practical political alternative. Arneson reported that after one meeting with Oppenheimer, Acheson quipped: "You know, I listened as carefully as I knew how, but I don't understand what 'Oppie' was trying to say. How can we persuade a paranoid adversary to disarm 'by example?' "[40] From where Acheson was sitting, and given his respon-

40. Acheson quoted in R. Gordon Arneson, "The H-Bomb Decision," *Foreign Service Journal*, XLVI (May, 1969), 29.

sibility, recommending against proceeding with the H-bomb project was simply not a viable alternative.

By the time the special committee met for the second (and last) time, on January 31, 1950, Acheson had made up his mind. He would cast his lot with Johnson, and the entire committee, including a reluctant Lilienthal, would sign a recommendation in favor of proceeding with the project. Yet it must be noted that Acheson was never truly aligned with Johnson; his vote on this issue was part of a larger plan. Like Kennan, Oppenheimer, and Lilienthal, Acheson wanted a review of all United States military strategy and policy—a review that no doubt would call for a build-up of conventional forces to complement a growing nuclear arsenal. Johnson, under severe budgetary pressures as he was, wanted no part of a review that was sure to upset the status quo at the Defense Department. Although Acheson found himself in something of an awkward position in voting for development, he did get the strategy and policy review he was seeking (later NSC-68).

The "moral argument" of Oppenheimer and Kennan continued to have some hold on Acheson, and it did help him hold out for the review he wanted, but this "non-communicable wisdom," as he called it, would never be sufficient to sway him to vote against the project. As Acheson himself put it, there were two pressing reasons why he could not allow the project to be delayed; "Our delaying research would not delay Soviet research, contrary to the initial hope I had briefly entertained"; and "the American people simply would not tolerate a policy of delaying nuclear research in so vital a matter while we sought for further ways of reaching accommodation with the Russians after the experiences of the years since the war." [41] The committee went directly to the White House with their recommendation, which the president immediately accepted.[42]

The only realist to oppose development outright was Kennan; the rest sided with Acheson, who in disagreeing with Kennan's "moral" argument thought that he could advance one of his own. Acheson's

41. Acheson, *Present at the Creation*, 349.
42. For more details on this episode, see David Lilienthal, *The Journals of David Lilienthal*, (7 vols., New York, 1964), II, esp. 630.

89

argument had less to do with political and bureaucratic pressure than with the belief that it was the government's solemn duty to protect its citizens. The United States government, according to this view, could not leave its citizens vulnerable in any way, even if protecting them meant developing weapons that it hoped never to have to use. As Morgenthau put it shortly after the H-bomb decision was made, "The modern state can no more afford to be without all the weapons which modern technology puts at its disposal than could the medieval knight afford to be without a sword."[43]

The realist position on the building of the H-bomb was based on a three-point strategy for establishing peace between the superpowers. First, the United States needed to build the H-bomb to maintain its status as the preeminent superpower; next, it had to shift its emphasis away from nuclear weapons, keeping them solely as a deterrent while building up conventional forces; finally, it had to work toward a comprehensive settlement with the Soviets over disputed territories in Europe, Asia, and the third world. The strategy was somewhat paradoxical in that it simultaneously called for the development of an H-bomb and emphasized a war-fighting strategy that would exclude this weapon. It was hoped that such a posture would show the Soviets that the United States had no designs to use the bomb as an offensive weapon. Acheson and Lippmann never went so far as to support a pledge of "no first use," as advocated by Kennan and Niebuhr, but they did believe that the only "use" for the H-bomb was as a deterrent.

In an early-February editorial in *Christianity and Crisis*, Niebuhr registered his opinion that "there can be only one justification for the development of this bomb and that is to prevent its use." He went on to endorse the proposal of pledging no first use as a way of further defining America's intentions. He reiterated, however, that the United States should make it clear that it would never suffer a failure of nerve when it came to protecting itself. "No nation," he wrote, "will fail to take even the most hazardous adventure into the future, if the alterna-

43. Hans Morgenthau, "The H-Bomb and After," *Bulletin of the Atomic Scientists*, VI (March, 1950), 76.

tive means the risk of being subjugated."[44] The United States, of course, was no exception.

Lippmann raised similar issues in his "Today and Tomorrow" column of February 2, 1950, "The Hydrogen Bomb." Like Kennan, he stressed the need for assessing "the relative value of this weapon among other weapons." Like all of the other realists, he disagreed with Nitze's opinion of nuclear weapons as "winning" weapons. "There could be no more grievous illusion," he wrote, "than to suppose that the hydrogen bomb will restore the balance of power on which so many of our calculations rested until September, 1949." With the atomic monopoly gone, no nuclear innovation could erase the fact that the Soviets possessed weapons sufficiently dangerous to threaten the United States regardless of American "superiority." There would have to be a change in attitude in the United States; the nation would have to recognize that it had been "fearfully misled and confused by the plausible fallacy of the military containment policy—a policy which was plausible because of our monopoly of atomic weapons."[45] The edge gained by building the H-bomb would not alter the fact that the Soviets were a formidable foe. The bomb would have to be built, but its "usefulness" was in doubt.

The next week Lippmann launched a scathing attack on the proponents of the project, especially Edward Teller, whom Lippmann rather sarcastically referred to as "Mr. T." It was not so much their position he was attacking—he agreed with proceeding with development—as it was their attitude. What bothered Lippmann about Teller and his associates was that they saw the building of the H-bomb as an end in itself, so that once construction was completed, "there is nothing further that can be done about it."[46] Lippmann believed that since the weapon should be built for deterrence, it must be viewed as a first

44. Reinhold Niebuhr, "Editorial Notes," *Christianity and Crisis*, X (February 20, 1950), 10–11.

45. Walter Lippmann, "The Hydrogen Bomb" ("Today and Tomorrow," February 2, 1950), in Lippmann Papers.

46. Walter Lippmann, "Mr. T. Thinks It Through" ("Today and Tomorrow," February 9, 1950), in Lippmann Papers.

step, not a last step. By itself, the building of the H-bomb was no way to establish a structure of peace. What followed the bomb's development would be most important, and Teller and his colleagues had little constructive to say about that.

Lippmann wrote that because the United States was "the first to make an atomic bomb, the first to use an atomic bomb, [and] the first to declare it will make a hydrogen bomb," it had a "peculiar and unavoidable and most solemn moral obligation to mankind." That moral obligation was "to search for a decent and honorable alternative to a war of extermination." Lippmann explained that Americans could not "sit down, fold their hands across their stomachs, saying that their search has ended, that they have reached the limits of their wisdom, and that there is nothing more they can do except to make more and better bombs." The "day we did that," he declared, "would mark the death of the American spirit."[47] It would be un-American—and morally reprehensible—to build such a weapon without trying to make it part of a comprehensive peace settlement.

One World or None

Lippmann himself could be accused of no such complacency. Along with the other realists, especially Acheson, he began the search for alternatives with a burst of enthusiasm. As early as 1946, the "logic" of deterrence already had disturbed the realists so much that it drove them to creative heights: they would not be satisfied with their own argument that the responsible thing to do, for the time being, was to threaten irresponsible acts.[48] "We have to realize that our progress in

47. *Ibid.*
48. It is interesting to note how the realists' view of deterrence presaged that of the Catholic bishops of the United States as expressed in their "Pastoral Letter on War and Peace" of May, 1983. The bishops' use of just-war theory in highlighting the importance of the *discriminate* use of force and the need for *proportionality* echoes the main tenets of the realists' guidelines for usable and unusable force. The bishops' "strictly conditioned" acceptance of deterrence as "a first step" toward peace and their call for a pledge of "no first use" are also similar to the positions that Kennan and Niebuhr held as early as 1950. These similarities illustrate just how important normative assumptions were for the re-

the art of mass destruction has not been accompanied by new discoveries in political science or statecraft," warned Lippmann.[49] He knew that this deficiency had to be addressed; something had to be done—even if it meant reshaping traditional assumptions about international agreements—so that the new weapons could be controlled.

The realists showed ingenuity and daring in their proposals. Lippmann offered his thoughts alongside analyses by Oppenheimer and others in the widely acclaimed *One World or None* (1946). Acheson made his presence felt by playing a major role in developing the official United States proposal for international control. He also headed the Acheson-Lilienthal committees that produced the blueprint for the Baruch Plan later presented at the United Nations.

Lippmann's article in *One World or None* and the Acheson-Lilienthal Report stood as evidence that the realists believed in arms control and that they were impelled toward this belief by their realization that atomic weapons were unlike any weapons they had seen before. The extraordinary nature of their proposals was a direct consequence of the extraordinary nature of the weapons themselves. Atomic monopoly or not, the realists were driven to solve the atomic dilemma before the arms race got into full gear. When the window of opportunity opened, they felt obliged to take advantage of it.

As the publication *One World or None* demonstrated, the realists were not alone on this issue.[50] A number of individuals and groups within the United States had settled on international control as the most desirable option and the logical place to start. The scientific community, and especially its members who had been associated with atomic research, were among the most vocal advocates of this ap-

---

alists, even in the early stages of their thinking about nuclear weapons. For more on the bishops' letter and deterrence, see Bruce Russett, "Ethics of Nuclear Deterrence," *International Security*, VIII (Spring, 1984), 36–54.

49. Walter Lippmann, "International Control of Atomic Energy," *One World or None*, ed. Dexter Masters (New York, 1946), 66.

50. See Paul Boyer, *By the Bomb's Early Light: American Thought and Culture at the Dawn of the Atomic Age* (New York, 1985), for a discussion of the circumstances surrounding the publication of *One World or None* and its public reception.

proach. In September, 1945, for instance, an influential group of scientists made their sentiments known to the public by releasing the previously confidential Franck Report. This report, submitted to the government the previous spring, had called upon President Truman not to use the atomic bomb on Japan without warning and to share atomic technology with the Soviets and other nations as part of an attempt to avoid an armaments race.

That same September, on the eighteenth, Acheson participated in an important cabinet meeting where there was sharp division on the issue of sharing secrets. Acheson sided with Stimson, who was about to retire from his post as secretary of war and who in preparation for the meeting had written a memo stating, among other things, that "if we fail to approach them [the Soviets] now and merely continue to negotiate with them, having this weapon rather ostentatiously on our hip, their suspicions and their distrust of our purposes and motives will increase."[51] Later, Acheson was given the assignment of following through on Stimson's line of thought and devising a plan that the Soviets could take seriously.

Acheson's substantive contributions were complemented by Lippmann's theoretical work. The great fear among some thinkers, as the title *One World or None* suggested, was that if a new world order were not achieved, the ultimate catastrophe could happen. Both Lippmann and Acheson saw the problem as one of sovereignty: as long as nations insisted upon having traditional, absolute sovereignty over atomic weapons, the world would not be truly safe. For if nations reserved the right (and ability) to develop and use atomic weapons unilaterally, any international agreement could be abrogated at will, and total destruction could result. The whole idea of sovereignty in this area needed rethinking. Atomic energy was a global resource with global implications. Its unique properties transcended national boundaries. On this occasion and on this issue, the national interest and the global interest seemed to be one and the same.

Lippmann's contribution to *One World or None* focused on the prob-

---

51. Henry Stimson quoted in Acheson, *Present at the Creation*, 123.

94

lem of how to create a supranational structure that could accommodate atomic energy. He theorized that the way to control atomic energy was to create a system that respected, but in effect superseded, traditional notions of sovereignty. The key to the system would be to make "individuals, not sovereign states, the objects of international agreements."[52] This innovation would allow for the establishment of universal laws and standards, which in turn would be implemented by each state. In this way each state still would be sovereign over its people, and states still would be the building blocks of international law. But all states would be working toward the same end; they would be in fundamental agreement on goals, and their laws would be designed to be consistent with those goals. By focusing on the individual as the target of law, Lippmann hoped to bypass the perils of obsessive national self-interest.

Under the proposed system, domestic legislation would be designed to coincide with laws set up by international agreements. Certain laws would cut across national boundaries, and in those areas where they did, each nation's laws would be consistent with other nations' laws so that there would be no conflict. Thus, by following the domestic law, each individual in effect would be following the universal, international law. There then would be a legal basis for the establishment of independent international agencies to control and direct all atomic research. Loyalty and the letter of the law would bind individuals to the international agency rather than to any single government.

For example, a scientist working on an atomic-energy project would be responsible to a universally agreed-upon body of law. His home country would have no special claim over his services; in fact, each country's laws would be written in such a way as to forbid it to interfere with such a person's work or enlist him in any secret project. There would arise a world-wide community of scientists devoted to the international development of atomic energy. These scientists' only allegiance would be to the international community under whose auspices

52. Lippmann, "International Control of Atomic Energy," in *One World or None*, ed. Masters, 68.

they worked. This arrangement, it was hoped, would kill the incentive of nations to compete, and put an end to the arms race. Knowledge and technology would be shared, and new bonds would be formed between individuals. These bonds would be based purely on interest in science. They would be fostered by natural intellectual curiosity and the wish to pursue research on the peaceful uses of atomic energy. Scientists no longer would be restricted by their country of origin; they would have their own global community.

In an unusual twist, Lippmann in effect called for a weakening of the nation-state. This is not what one ordinarily would expect from a realist. Where in this scheme, one might ask, was the hallmark of realism, "national interest defined in terms of power"? With his proposal, Lippmann seemed to be a realist in retreat. This was not the case. Lippmann still was concerned with interest and power; however, he questioned whether holding on to the atomic monopoly, short-lived as it was bound to be, necessarily would enhance the interests of the United States. He speculated that the national interest in this case might be served best by the supranational structure he envisioned.

Even more unusual was Lippmann's assessment of where responsibility should lie in the atomic age. Writing during the time of the Nuremberg trials, he could not help despairing of the current system of sovereignty and loyalty for its failure. The war-crimes trials proved to him that statesmen frequently acted with no regard for higher law; their ultimate loyalty was to their own state. Lippmann saw this as a dangerous situation that could not be tolerated, especially in a world with atomic weapons. This conviction led him to do what the Nuremberg justices had done: to focus on individuals as the source of responsibility in the world—individuals responsible to one another and not solely to their nation-states.

In all of this Lippmann grasped at restoring a moral dimension to the struggle for power. Quoting Justice Robert H. Jackson's words from the Nuremberg trials, Lippmann wrote that it was necessary to take "the ultimate step," which is "to make statesmen responsible to law." [53] Lippmann never wholly escaped the early influence that Woodrow Wil-

53. *Ibid.*, 71.

son had exerted on him; he still held on to a hope for a universal world order based on international law and agreements. In *One World or None*, he painted a picture that bordered on utopian. But like all realists, he had to have an ideal toward which to strive. Lippmann's contribution to *One World or None* is best understood as his articulation of that ideal, complete with the practical steps needed to reach it.

Far from being a realist in retreat, Lippmann in 1946 gave voice to the very essence of postwar American realism. He perceived national interest in its broadest sense, as it related to power and responsibility. If this meant that in dealing with atomic energy an emphasis had to be placed on the supranational rather than the national, then so be it. The national interest was not always served by the accumulation of more and more power. For this brief moment in 1946, Lippmann thought that the national interest would be served best and power be used most responsibly if international control could be achieved. He proved that a realist does not always advise his nation to try to outmuscle its opponent. Where interests coincide and common ground can be found, business can and should be done.

Getting that business done was the job given to Acheson and David Lilienthal in 1946. Acheson had made his opinions known in late September, 1945, in a memo to President Truman in which Acheson had stated his belief that the atomic monopoly would be short-lived and that the United States should push for an agreement with the Soviets and the British on international control. Characteristically, Acheson wanted the agreement to be worked out among the great powers themselves. He believed that the United Nations, chock full of small, powerless nations with wildly divergent interests, was no place to broker such a deal. Acheson hoped that the great powers could work out on their own an agreement that would provide for an exchange of scientific information and address the problem of inspection.[54] These basic ideas would be the starting point for the Acheson-Lilienthal committees.

Among Acheson's committee members were some of the leading

54. Dean Acheson, "Memo to Truman" (September, 1945), in U.S. Department of State, *Foreign Relations of the United States, 1945* (9 vols.; Washington, D.C., 1967), II, 48–50.

97

figures of the military-industrial-governmental establishment: Vannevar Bush, president of the Carnegie Institution and director of the Office of Scientific Research; James B. Conant, president of Harvard University; General Leslie Groves, commandant of the Manhattan Project; and John J. McCloy, former assistant secretary of war. On the board of consultants, chaired by Lilienthal, were Oppenheimer, former director of the Los Alamos Atomic Laboratory; Charles A. Thomas, vice-president of Monsanto Chemical; and Henry A. Winne, vice-president of General Electric. Clearly, Acheson intended to bring to the task as much prestige, knowledge, and experience as possible. After being "tutored" by the specialists on the peculiar properties of atomic energy, Acheson and his colleagues spent four days in March at the Dumbarton Oaks mansion in Washington working out a framework for international control.

The task was a delicate one: the potential for domestic political disaster was as threatening as the danger from overseas. Giving up the monopoly, even in a slow, methodical fashion, was bound to cause anxieties within the United States. Acutely aware of this, the drafters of the committees' report tried to make it clear that the United States would receive something in return for its magnanimity: increased security. As Acheson stated at the time: "In plain words, the Report sets up a plan under which no nation would make atomic bombs or materials for them. All dangerous activities would be carried on—not merely inspected—by a live, functioning international Authority with a real purpose in the world capable of attracting competent personnel." [55] Because the international authority would be invested with so much power, it would suffer none of the indignities, nor be as impotent, as other international organizations such as the League of Nations or the UN.

Unfortunately—from Acheson's point of view—Truman decided to ignore his advice about negotiating directly with the Soviets. The president would put the proposal before the UN and attempt to work within the UN system. Worse still for Acheson was Truman's decision

55. Acheson, *Present at the Creation,* 153.

to appoint financier Bernard Baruch as the presenter of the proposal. Acheson thought Baruch to be a self-promoter and a man generally ill-suited for the complex art of diplomacy. It was not long before the two clashed. Baruch insisted that any agreement would have to provide for sanctions or even "swift and sure" punishment in the event of a violation. Acheson and his committee had decided that such calls for punitive measures "were very dangerous words that added nothing to a treaty and were almost certain to wreck any possibility of a Russian acceptance of one." [56] As it turned out, Acheson's assessment was correct. The Soviets would not sign an agreement that allowed for sanctions or punishment, nor would they agree to Baruch's demand that the Great Power veto in the Security Council of the UN *not* apply to atomic matters.

Acheson and Baruch did agree on one thing: the United States should not give up its monopoly without absolute assurance that an agreement could be verified and enforced. The political and strategic issues that separated the United States and the Soviet Union were formidable, but no single issue separated them more than the general problem of distrust. Baruch's tough talk alone did not kill the prospects for a treaty; given the attitudes and passions of the rival governments, it may have been impossible to consummate an agreement. The Soviets would never agree to a plan that would deny them atomic weapons while the Americans retained theirs, and the United States would not relinquish the monopoly until it could be absolutely sure that the Soviets could not gain an upper hand in an eventual arms race.[57] For all their trying, neither side came close to finding acceptable terms. Neither side was able to figure out a way to transcend its parochial national interest. Neither could trust that the other would consider its national interest and the global interest to be one and the same in the matter of atomic energy.

Under these circumstances, it did not take long for both sides to stop trying to work out a compromise. Acheson, like many others, saw

56. *Ibid.*, 155.
57. Gaddis Smith, *Dean Acheson* (New York, 1972), 384.

that the United States was unlikely to get an agreement that met its standards, and he stated his opinion that the country would be better off without an agreement than with a flawed one. The Soviets appeared to feel the same way. They, too, were unwilling to settle for a deal that, from their perspective, was flawed. Both sides recognized that they had reached an impasse. Writing in an effort to come to terms with the death of the Baruch Plan, Lippmann stated his belief that "in discussing armaments with the Russians we ought to talk privately, and only at the highest level, and only when we are in sight of a general settlement in Europe, the Middle East and the Far East." Until then, he concluded, "no one is going to disarm anyway and we ought not to disarm." [58]

This was the position of all the realists; if the Soviets would not accept the Baruch Plan and would not move toward a general settlement of postwar disputes, then disarmament should not even be considered. As far as the realists were concerned, Soviet intransigence, combined with the predictable futility of negotiating through the UN, had made the collapse of the deal palatable and even attractive. The skepticism of Acheson and Lippmann began to match that of Kennan's Long Telegram, and their thoughts moved with renewed emphasis to the protection of specifically American interests.

In a 1948 editorial, Niebuhr claimed that "one world or none" was a "foolish slogan." It was foolish, he wrote, "because any sober analysis of the contemporary scene must convince an honest student of the present of the impossibility of achieving world government." Acheson and Lippmann never were enamored with the notion of world federalism either, even though they favored a limited form of it in the idea of international control. By 1948, however, the idea of moving toward *any* form of world government seemed dangerously naïve to them, whether such a move were limited to backing an atomic regulatory agency or expanded to full-fledged support of the UN or a world state. The realists lined up behind Niebuhr, who believed "mankind is

58. Walter Lippmann, "Secrecy and Inspection" ("Today and Tomorrow," November 23, 1946), in Lippmann Papers.

fated to live many decades and possibly for generations in a world which ought to be one but cannot become one."[59] The realists truly wanted a global order, especially when it came to atomic weapons, but they had learned through experience that it would not be easily or quickly accomplished. They could only conclude that as desirable as the "one world or none" slogan might sound, those who still were peddling it in 1948 were the most dangerous of fools.

Massive Retaliation and the Arms Race

If One Worlders were fools on the left, then the practitioners of "brinkmanship" were fools on the right. Both groups felt the unremitting sting of realist criticism; both were deemed dangerous and irresponsible. As the cold war dragged on through the 1950s, the realists turned their barbs increasingly toward Secretary of State John Foster Dulles, the chief architect of Eisenhower's foreign policy through most of the president's two terms. Dulles' initiative known as the "New Look," his strategy of "massive retaliation," and his calls for the "rollback" of Communist gains were met with disdain. As strongly as the realists were advocating a hard line against Communist aggression (and the threat of further aggression, originating primarily from the Soviet Union), they nevertheless found Dulles' approach immoral, impractical, and wrong-headed.

Dulles did not recoil from nuclear weapons in the same instinctive way as the realists. He saw in these weapons a potential for both actual and threatened use, whereas the realists were more skeptical and wary. Instead of discussing disarmament or at least a deemphasis on nuclear forces in America's defense posture, Dulles proposed that nuclear weapons be at the center of the nation's military strategy and foreign policy. He saw the weapons as America's strength: they were both the winning weapon and the potential source of tremendous political leverage. Not only that, but they were also economically efficient, especially when compared with the costs of maintaining large conventional

59. Reinhold Niebuhr, "One World or None," *Christianity and Crisis*, VIII (February 16, 1948), 9.

101

armies. Dulles' New Look featured an increased reliance on nuclear weapons and a reduced dependence on conventional forces. The result would be "a bigger bang for the buck"—more firepower at lower cost, fewer men needed to stand guard in Germany and at other points around the globe. On the domestic political front, the New Look had its share of attractions.[60]

The military strategy that went along with the New Look became known as "massive retaliation." First unveiled in an article in *Life* magazine during the 1952 presidential campaign, massive retaliation was explained as "*the means to retaliate instantly against open aggression by Red Armies, so that, if it occurred anywhere, we could and we would strike back where it hurts, by means of our own choosing.*"[61] Under this doctrine the United States would reserve to itself a certain flexibility in responding to Communist aggression. If, for example, the Soviets threatened Western Europe, they would face the possibility—or probability—that the United States would retaliate by striking Soviet targets on Soviet territory. Such retaliation conceivably could include the use of nuclear weapons. The choice of targets and the timing of the attack would not be required to bear any direct relationship to the aggressive act that prompted the response. "The principle involved is as simple as that of our mutual police forces," wrote Dulles. "We do not station armed guards at every house to stop aggressors—that would be economic suicide—but we deter potential aggressors by making it probable that if they aggress, they will lose in punishment more than they can gain by aggression."[62]

While Eisenhower and Dulles implemented their "Policy of Boldness," they also were taking the relatively passive concept of containment and turning it into an active policy of "liberation" or "rollback." This did not bother the realists so much as the overall change in military tactics that the Eisenhower-Dulles foreign policy seemed to de-

---

60. For more on Dulles and his vision of military strategy and diplomacy in the 1950s, see Townsend Hoopes, *The Devil and John Foster Dulles* (Boston, 1973).

61. John Foster Dulles, "A Policy of Boldness," *Life*, XXXII (May 19, 1952), 151. Emphasis his.

62. *Ibid.*

mand. The realists believed that the choice to promote nuclear weapons over conventional weapons was a mistake, as was the rigid posture of confrontation and the stated willingness to go to the brink. For all of its flexibility in the choosing of timing and targets, massive retaliation did more to restrict the options available to the statesman than it did to offer him new ones. Morgenthau felt that Dulles' scheme narrowed the choices for policy to a point where the United States must either risk all-out atomic war or be rendered impotent.[63] The lack of an intermediate option—the capacity to wage a limited war for limited purposes—put the United States in a precarious position.

Massive retaliation committed the United States to an all-or-nothing strategy that the realists could not accept. Brinkmanship could not be practiced indefinitely; sooner or later, someone was bound to call the bluff. The lack of flexibility created a dual danger: minor conflicts could escalate into dangerous confrontations, or a "new pacifism" could emerge wherein the United States would back away from conflict in order to avoid an unpredictable all-or-nothing situation.[64] The search for a middle ground between massive retaliation and the possible emergence of a new pacifism was resolved in part by the publication of Henry Kissinger's *Nuclear Weapons and Foreign Policy* in 1957. Kissinger's position—that the United States should develop the capability to fight limited wars with small, tactical nuclear weapons—was well received. Although the realists later became troubled by the concept of limited nuclear war, in 1957 they welcomed this alternative to the threat of total destruction and hailed the new direction popularized by Kissinger.

Kissinger's ideas took into account the need to be able to defend American interests by fighting wars that would not necessarily escalate into Armageddon. Reviewing Kissinger's book, Niebuhr wrote, "We must be ready to fight limited wars in terms of our objectives and to

63. Hans Morgenthau, "The Political and Military Strategy of the U.S.," *Bulletin of the Atomic Scientists*, X (October, 1954), 323–27.

64. See Hans Morgenthau, "Atomic Force and American Foreign Policy," *Commentary*, XXIII (June, 1957), 501–505. See also Dean Acheson, "The Instant Retaliation Debate Continued," *New York Times Magazine*, March 28, 1954, pp. 13, 77–78.

win them with appropriate weapons." The "appropriate weapons" in this case were tactical nuclear weapons; they were preferable to the more indiscriminate, more destructive, and less controllable strategic nuclear weapons that formed the backbone of massive retaliation. Even Kennan, an ardent critic of all nuclear weapons, wrote at the time that a move toward tactical nuclear arms was "a step in the right direction." [65] Niebuhr concluded his review by declaring Kissinger's book a "circumspect and wise analysis," one that "makes more sense than anything which has come to our notice in recent times." [66]

Kissinger's book made "more sense" because it restored the direct correlation between ends and means in the use of force. Unlike massive retaliation, in which the threat of force was not directly related and was therefore potentially disproportionate to the objective sought, Kissinger's strategy called for a clear, measured use of force brought to bear directly upon the objective. There would be more control over the force employed, and it could be increased or decreased depending on the circumstances.

This was arguably a more responsible approach to the use of power than the one advocated by Dulles. It was a far cry from disarmament or arms control, but at least it was an effort to *control* the use of force. For the time being, the answer to Dulles' "irresponsibility" was reliance on tactical nuclear weapons and an increase in conventional military capability. This appeared to the realists to be the best way to bring the responsible use of force back into the nation's military strategy.

The "irresponsible" nature of Dulles' New Look, however, was not limited to strategic issues. It had broad implications for all of American society. The realists' criticism of the New Look extended to its effects on the nation's economy and social structure. The realists already were worried about the "military-industrial complex" when President Eisenhower coined the term in his Farewell Address in 1961. Speaking to the nation just before his departure from office, Eisenhower said: "This conjunction of an immense military establishment and large in-

65. George Kennan, *Russia, the Atom, and the West* (New York, 1957), 58.
66. Reinhold Niebuhr, "Limited Warfare," *Christianity and Crisis*, XVII (November 11, 1957), 147.

dustry is new in the American experience. The total influence—economic, political, even spiritual—is felt in every city, every State house, every office of the Federal government. We recognize the imperative need for this development. Yet we must not fail to comprehend its grave implications. Our toil, resources, and livelihood are all involved; so is the very structure of our society." [67] Despite the administration's "bigger bang for the buck" policies, the large military budget was cause for great concern. There was a tightening link between the military services, which spent huge amounts of government money, and the giant corporations that researched, designed, and built military hardware, and this alliance was changing the face of the economy. These developments made many people—not just the realists—uneasy.

In addition to being disconcerting, the situation was puzzling. Large amounts of money were being spent to build heavy weapons, yet the nation seemed to be growing less secure. After *Sputnik* in 1957, it was clear that despite all United States efforts, the Soviets had gained an advantage in at least one phase of the arms race. Something had gone wrong in the 1950s. Government money had created and was sustaining a self-perpetuating military-industrial behemoth, yet in the process the United States appeared to be losing ground to the Soviets. The United States had plenty of missiles, but they were proving to be of dubious value in places such as Indochina, places that had become the new battlegrounds of the cold war. On top of this, there were even suggestions of a "missile gap." By 1960 there were worries about inflation, and the Soviets looked like formidable opponents in what Lippmann termed "the coming tests with Russia" around the globe. Perhaps, in spite of all of its intentions of providing a fiscally responsible policy while maintaining a strong deterrent to Soviet adventurism in the third world, the New Look needed to be revised.

How had the United States come to this pass? The realists had their own theory. "What is happening," wrote Lippmann, "is that under the leadership of the President [Eisenhower] we are promoting private

67. Dwight D. Eisenhower, *Public Papers of the Presidents of the United States: Dwight D. Eisenhower, 1960–1961* (Washington, D.C., 1961), 1036–41.

105

prosperity at the expense of national power." As a result, Lippmann concluded, "the influence of the United States is declining."[68] Later he would write, "Such philistinism and materialism are the attributes of a second-rate power, and they are our real cause for concern (not just the so-called missile gap or deterrence gap)."[69]

American society, according to Lippmann, had lost its will to fight the good fight. It had grown soft in the sense that it had "become fat with consumer goods" and enamored with private prosperity. As early as 1957 Lippmann had observed, "Surely the reason that the Soviet Union is ahead of us in the missiles is, first, that her efforts are concentrated while ours have been dispersed, and second, that the Soviet Union has put not only defense but science and public education above a high standard of public consumption."[70] In 1960 he still maintained this interpretation: America was fat, happy, and acting irresponsibly by committing itself to a wide network of alliances without providing the forces necessary to back up those commitments.

Realist criticism reflected the double bind facing the United States at the end of the 1950s. On the one hand, there was great fear of a military build-up based on nuclear weapons. On the other hand, there was an even greater fear of a missile gap that would give the Soviets strategic superiority. In some respects American society seemed too nonchalant about its defense, while in others it seemed to be falling victim to the military-industrial complex it had created.

The realists offered their suggestions for remedies: First, the United States had to make up its mind to counter the Soviet missile threat, and promptly allocate resources for the necessary research and development. Second, once parity was achieved, international agreements should be pursued to slow down the impractical arms race. The realists had concluded that the United States was spending too much

68. Walter Lippmann, "A Satisfied Nation" ("Today and Tomorrow," January 21, 1960), in Lippmann Papers.
69. Walter Lippmann, "Weapons and Space" ("Today and Tomorrow," January 26, 1960), in Lippmann Papers.
70. Walter Lippmann, "The President's Speeches" ("Today and Tomorrow," November 7, 1957), in Lippmann Papers.

money on weapons that would not be used. Anything that slowed the arms race would be helpful, and as soon as the United States could bargain from a situation of strength, it *should* bargain. Eventually, after the Cuban missile crisis and a look into the abyss of what massive retaliation might have wrought, the realists and the rest of the nation turned to the idea of a test ban and other methods of controlling nuclear weapons.

The Test Ban, ABM, SALT, and After

The idea of banning tests of nuclear weapons was nothing new in 1963, when the first nuclear test ban treaty was signed. Rather, agreement on the Atmospheric Test Ban Treaty of 1963 followed years of acrimonious debate and frustrating negotiation. Throughout the 1950s, interest in a test ban treaty waxed and waned with political and scientific developments. After H-bomb tests by both the United States and the Soviet Union resulted in global fears about radioactive fallout, popular opinion in the United States began to favor a test ban. Yet in the wake of the Soviet advances symbolized by the success of *Sputnik*, significant countervailing domestic pressure rose within the United States against the idea of a test ban. This tug of war continued into the 1960s as political leaders and scientists debated the merits of a test ban and contemplated the feasibility of reaching and enforcing any such agreement.[71]

The realists favored the idea of a test ban treaty on two grounds: first, it could help slow down the expensive arms race; second, it was necessary to protect the environment. The realists' support of a ban was tempered, however, by their concerns about verification and the need for the United States to retain enough military power to protect its vital interests. In short, the realists generally favored the idea of a test ban throughout the 1950s, but they never saw it as the single most important issue to be negotiated between the United States and the Soviet Union. It had the potential to be a useful tool, and it could be

71. For an excellent history of test ban politics, see Robert Divine, *Blowing on the Wind: The Nuclear Test Ban Debate, 1945–1960* (New York, 1978).

107

mutually beneficial. But a test ban treaty, like any arms-control measure, could be only *part* of the solution to international conflict, not the solution itself.

Kennan entered the debate in the fall of 1956, just before the presidential election of that year. In a letter to the editor of the New York *Times*, Kennan lent his support to the Democratic nominee, Adlai Stevenson, who had called for a halt to the testing of large nuclear devices "conditional upon adherence by the other atomic powers to a similar policy." [72] Kennan questioned the military necessity of continuing with H-bomb testing and accused the Eisenhower administration of ignoring world opinion, which was heavily against further testing.

"A sizable portion of the world's population," Kennan wrote, "views these experiments, rightly or wrongly, with horror and misgiving and already tends to attribute to them a wide variety of human ills, including the weather. If the administration is at all concerned about this, it has not shown it." To Kennan, it was frustrating that the administration had shown "no hint of a readiness to explore whatever helpful possibilities might reside in Mr. Stevenson's suggestion." This insensitivity and closed-mindedness were making ever more remote the possibility of reducing tensions and insuring a safer environment through a test ban." [73]

The same week that Kennan's letter was printed, Lippmann weighed in with a similar opinion in his regular "Today and Tomorrow" column. Like Kennan, Lippmann agreed with Stevenson's suggestion that the United States negotiate a test ban treaty; he cited the danger of fallout as the principal reason. Lippmann believed a test ban to be feasible, verifiable, and enforceable: "An international treaty to suspend the testing of bombs big enough to be detected abroad, big enough therefore to pollute the air abroad, would—if it were properly negotiated—stand no greater chance of being violated than any of our other agreements—for example, the agreement which enables us to

72. Adlai Stevenson quoted in Divine, *Blowing on the Wind*, 87.
73. George Kennan, "To Ban the H-Bomb Tests," New York *Times*, October 28, 1956, Sec. 4, p. 10.

stay in West Berlin." In sum, the collective benefits of a ban seemed to outnumber its potential dangers. It was a step worth taking.[74]

Four years later, with little or no progress made toward an agreement, Lippmann still believed it was a step worth taking. In fact, he saw it as such an important step that he urged policy makers to end their quest for a perfect agreement and accept a treaty that might be imperfect but was at least a step in the direction of peaceful coexistence. Lippmann challenged the assumption that "no treaty is better than an imperfect treaty," that is, that the United States should sign a test ban agreement only if it were 100 percent certain that it was verifiable. Lippmann argued for more flexibility on the American side, including recognition that the Soviets were proposing significant concessions (in 1960) on issues such as inspection. He speculated that if only the United States would bend a little, an agreement might be reached. Such an agreement might not provide ironclad security, but that would not be its purpose. Its purpose would be to register changes in the Soviet system, for example, the installation of inspection stations manned by foreigners on Soviet territory. If American negotiators could extract an agreement like that out of the Soviets, Lippmann believed it was worth serious consideration.[75]

Acheson did not see it that way at all. He feared that practically any agreement that could possibly be reached with the Soviets in the late 1950s "would be disadvantageous to us and would not diminish the chance of nuclear war." He found the possibility of reaching an agreement more threatening than living without one. What concerned him most was strengthening "American and British nuclear power located in Europe, as well as allied (including American) conventional forces and tactical air power." The quest for a test ban, Acheson thought, was detracting from efforts to solve the more pressing problem of defending Europe and other American interests. To him, a test ban was a

74. Walter Lippmann, "The H-Bomb Tests" ("Today and Tomorrow," October 25, 1956), in Lippmann Papers.

75. Walter Lippmann, "Nuclear Testing," ("Today and Tomorrow," February 12, 1960), in Lippmann Papers.

matter of "secondary importance."[76] Not only had it received more attention than it deserved throughout the 1950s, but if it were taken seriously, it could even damage the nation's security.

The other realists also considered a test ban to be of secondary importance, but they did not relegate it to the distant background as Acheson did. Whereas he remained fixated on danger, they preferred to hold out hope. That hope reached its height in the summer of 1963 with the signing of the Atmospheric Test Ban Treaty. For the most part, the treaty was viewed as a great achievement. It was heartening that even after years of stalled negotiations and bickering, the United States and the Soviet Union were able to find enough common ground on which to base even a limited test ban treaty. Niebuhr praised the agreement for its potentially beneficial effects on the environment and for its part in reducing tensions among the great powers.[77] Lippmann, after wholeheartedly endorsing the Kennedy administration's efforts in negotiating the treaty, marveled that the agreement "sounds too good to be true."[78]

Lippmann was most excited about the treaty because it appeared to signal the end of an era in which nations searched for an "absolute weapon." Continued nuclear testing and development had been driven largely by the desire to invent such a weapon—one capable of annihilating an opponent and against which no defense existed. Even if both sides had given up their desire to develop an absolute weapon for their own purposes, each still would have been forced to continue the search for fear that the other would invent an invulnerable weapon first. The first step toward ending the arms race was to break the cycle of fear by recognizing that the pursuit of an absolute weapon was a mutual mistake that fueled a never-ending quest for superiority. If both sides

76. Dean Acheson, *Power and Diplomacy* (Cambridge, Mass., 1958), 103; see also Acheson, "NATO and Nuclear Weapons," *New Republic*, CXXXVII (December 30, 1957), 16.

77. Reinhold Niebuhr, "Test Ban Agreement," *Christianity and Crisis*, XXIII (September 16, 1963), 155.

78. Walter Lippmann, "The President and the Cold War" ("Today and Tomorrow," June 13, 1963), in Lippmann Papers.

would give up the search for the ultimate weapon, the gadget that would give its possessor the permanent upper hand, then the arms race could be abandoned. The test ban, Lippmann hoped, was a signal that the superpowers had renounced their search for an absolute weapon and that they were willing to live in a world of nuclear parity based on deterrence.

It is more likely, however, that the United States and the Soviet Union were looking for some form of temporary reprieve from the costly, tense arms race rather than for a permanent commitment to refrain from research and development. After all, the treaty represented a *limited* test ban, barring atmospheric testing only, and neither side suspended its development programs. Even in their excitement, realists like Lippmann saw plenty to temper their enthusiasm; indeed, it was their reservations, more than anything else, that distinguished the realists from other supporters of the treaty. It was not that the realists were looking for a black cloud; it was just that they were instinctively wary of anything that looked "too good to be true."

Morgenthau warned that the excessive excitement and increased expectations that inevitably arise after agreements like the test ban treaty could be a problem. He cited the "euphoric intervals" following Chamberlain's meeting with Hitler at Munich in 1938 and Khrushchev's visit to the United States in 1959 as examples of historical moments when raised hopes got in the way of clear thinking. As much as the relief offered by the treaty pleased him, he could not approach Great Power relations in the wake of the agreement with unfettered optimism.

"The limited test ban treaty," he wrote, "transforms into a temporary multilateral obligation the technological necessity, which had previously been observed by nuclear powers unilaterally, to stop testing for a considerable period of time after the completion of a series of tests."[79] Morgenthau had only the lowest of expectations from the treaty. These expectations eventually were exceeded, but his message

79. Hans Morgenthau, "Peace in Our Time?" *Commentary*, XXXVII (March, 1964), 67.

was no less clear: the treaty had not changed the fundamental relationship between the United States and other nations with nuclear capability, and it should not be interpreted as if it had. For Morgenthau and all the realists, the test ban treaty was something to applaud but nothing to get overexcited about.

Lippmann's analysis, even in its most optimistic moments, reflected this sobriety. In a column entitled "The First Step and the Second," written in July, 1963, Lippmann called attention to the fact that the test ban was only a "first step." Any first step, he claimed, merely suggests a direction; after that step is taken, there are many different ways to proceed in that general direction.[80] These thoughts were echoed by Niebuhr two months later: "The basic question concerns the next step, since everyone assures us that this is only the first step in relaxing Cold War tensions." Niebuhr spoke for all the realists when he concluded, "Clearly, the next step will be much more difficult."[81]

Niebuhr's prediction was accurate: the next step did prove to be more difficult. During the next decade the superpowers stumbled along in efforts to follow up on their 1963 breakthrough. The only success of the late 1960s was the nonproliferation treaty of 1968, in which the United States, Great Britain, and the Soviet Union (France and the People's Republic of China refused to sign) agreed to keep nuclear technology out of the hands of non-nuclear states. The limited success of that treaty was followed four years later, in 1972, by the signing of the ABM (antiballistic missile) treaty and the SALT I (Strategic Arms Limitations Talks) agreements.

The nonproliferation treaty, the ABM treaty, and the SALT I agreements, as important as they were, provided only temporary, limited, and sometimes ineffective injunctions against the arms race. The overwhelming trend during the late 1960s and early 1970s continued to be toward developing ever more sophisticated weapons systems. All of these treaties, along with the SALT II agreement negotiated under

80. Walter Lippmann, "The First Step and the Second" ("Today and Tomorrow," July 30, 1963), in Lippmann Papers.
81. Niebuhr, "Test Ban Agreement," 155.

President Carter, were conceived to stem the tide of the new technologies—but the new technologies were not that easy to control.

A prime example of a new technology that needed to be regulated was the antiballistic missile defense system that was being developed in the early 1970s. If perfected, such a system could have altered the strategic nuclear balance between the United States and the Soviet Union by providing a safety net—or rather, an overhead shield—for the cities or missile-launching sites it protected. The ABM defensive concept envisioned using guided missiles to destroy incoming ballistic missiles before they reached their intended targets. From a military standpoint, the ABM system was attractive: it finally promised a defense that had been lacking in the nuclear age, and it made retaliatory capability almost certain. The system presented several troublesome features, however: not only could it upset the existing balance of power, but it also opened up an entirely new area of weapons competition— and it was extremely expensive. All the realists, with the exception of Acheson, considered the system to be more trouble than it was worth. Most of them were pleased to see the ABM treaty signed; they believed that ABMs could use some regulating and limiting in their deployment—especially since the Soviets were ahead in this area.

Morgenthau rejected the concept of an ABM defense on the grounds that "it is hardly worth having if it is not very close to 100 percent effective." The very idea of strategic defense where nuclear weapons were concerned struck him as mistaken. Since a small number of missiles could inflict unacceptable damage, any system that could not offer something approaching total invulnerability was of little value. In the nuclear world, the only sure defense was through deterrence—and antinuclear missiles were more apt to undermine deterrence than strengthen it.

Morgenthau thought that an ABM system "could be destabilizing by creating the illusion that one side has a defensive advantage which would let them use force without risking unacceptable damage in retaliation." It seemed to him that the proponents of the defensive system were thinking about nuclear war in conventional terms. They did not

113

recognize that the margin of superiority they were seeking by implementing this defense was meaningless and that their illusions about gaining the phantom advantage could only lead to disaster.[82]

Realists like Morgenthau saw the ABM system as part of the pursuit of the absolute weapon, the pursuit Lippmann had feared so much in the early 1960s. This long-standing fear surfaced every time a new weapons system threatened to take the arms race across a new threshold. For the most part, the realists argued against any extension of the arms race. A prescient Kennan wrote in 1954:

> What sort of life is it to which these devotees of the weapons race would see us condemned? The technological realities of this competition are constantly changing from month to month and from year to year. Are we to flee like haunted creatures from one defensive device to another, each more costly and humiliating than the one before, cowering underground one day, breaking up our cities the next, attempting to surround ourselves with elaborate electronic shields on the third, concerned only to prolong the length of our lives while sacrificing all the values for which it might be worthwhile to live at all?[83]

In referring to electronic shields raised out of fear, Kennan could have been writing about 1972 or 1983 instead of 1954. The basic issue— whether manifested in the development of strategic nuclear weapons, the ABM system, or SDI (Strategic Defense Initiative)—was the same in each of those years: Would the United States and the Soviet Union draw a line against the advancement of new weapons systems? Or would they continue the competition, creating new fields upon which to compete?

Acheson alone had a fundamentally different view of the ABM. He believed that the system had to be developed for the same reason the H-bomb had to be developed: the Soviets must not be allowed a monopoly on a device that could give them a potentially decisive advantage. Acheson's strong feelings on the subject led him into the heated

82. Hans Morgenthau, *A New Foreign Policy for the United States* (New York, 1969), 229–30.
83. Kennan, *Russia, the Atom, and the West,* 54.

public debate over the ABM in 1969. His statements in support of ABM development and deployment were among his last political efforts before his death in 1971. Appearing on the nationally televised "David Frost Show" in debate with Senator Charles Percy of Illinois, Acheson warned: "Science is moving very fast. But you cannot turn over the whole field of development to the opponent with any degree of safety." Acheson reiterated that the United States had no alternative to development. "One must stay with it, Mr. Frost," he said to the moderator. "One has to stay all the time with it. If you delay and delay, and the other person experiments and develops and develops, you are losing ground." [84]

Whereas Senator Percy wanted to draw the line against further development, Acheson felt obliged to keep up with the adversary. The frightening costs of development and deployment, which Percy argued were prohibitive, did not deter Acheson at all. Money, in this case, was of secondary importance; it was a sacrifice America had to be willing to make. In an article published in the Washington *Star* two weeks after his television appearance, Acheson called the ABM project a "comparatively small investment" that "buys added security for a large portion of our retaliatory force." Acheson was seduced by the idea of a nuclear shield. "The ABM will not hurt anyone," he wrote. "It will not enter Soviet territory. It is designed to meet and destroy an offensive weapon in space or above our territory." [85] All things considered, Acheson found the ABM system to be a reasonable proposition.

Acheson stood alone among the realists on this matter precisely because he continued to think about nuclear weapons in conventional terms. The other realists, especially Morgenthau, refused to take seriously the notion of defensive weapons systems designed to stop nuclear attacks. This sort of thinking, according to Morgenthau, was symptomatic of what was wrong with arms control as the United States

84. "The David Frost Show: ABM Discussion with Dean Acheson and Charles Percy," July 15, 1969, transcript in Box 54, Dean Acheson Papers, Yale University, New Haven.
85. Dean Acheson, "A Citizen Takes a Hard Look at the ABM Debate," Washington *Star*, July 27, 1969, copy in Box 54, Acheson Papers.

115

and the Soviet Union were pursuing it. In regard to the SALT negotiations still going on in 1979, Morgenthau wrote, "They have bargained and haggled for seven years over issues that may be relevant for conventional weapons but most of which are certainly irrelevant for the nuclear field." Referring to the MIRV (multiple independently targeted reentry vehicle) controversy, which plagued the negotiations for some time, Morgenthau was dismissive: "As long as the number of warheads does not affect the mutual ability of assured destruction . . . the quantity of the mutual means of destruction is irrelevant."[86] Morgenthau saw the controversy over MIRVs and how they should be counted as further evidence that the negotiators continued to think about nuclear weapons in outmoded conventional terms. As far as he was concerned, painstakingly counting warheads, like developing a new defense system, was of dubious merit. Both pursuits smacked of old-fashioned reasoning.

In spite of his criticisms, Morgenthau endorsed the SALT process. He found the SALT I talks and the Interim Agreement on Offensive Missiles that came out of them to be useful because they at least worked to stabilize "the quantity of nuclear weapons" while allowing for "their qualitative improvement."[87] The agreement, "interim" though it was, represented a small step in a positive direction. "SALT II," Morgenthau wrote in 1979, "in spite of its conceptual confusion, is the practical precondition for SALT III to be built on a sounder intellectual basis providing for more tangible steps toward nuclear arms control and disarmament."[88] For him, as for most of the realists, negotiations and agreements like SALT had to be endorsed if only because they were what arms control was all about: small steps toward peaceful coexistence.

Kennan registered a similar opinion on the SALT process: he considered it to be "good, so far as it goes," but he thought it "unlikely to be enough." Like Morgenthau, he criticized the negotiators for their

86. Hans Morgenthau, "The Dilemma of SALT," *Newsletter: National Commission on American Foreign Policy,* II (August, 1979), copy in Box 109, Hans Morgenthau Papers, University of Virginia, Charlottesville.
87. Morgenthau, *Politics Among Nations* (1985), 441.
88. Morgenthau, "Dilemma of SALT."

lack of creativity. "So long as the view prevails," he wrote, "that the party has won the SALT talks which has contrived to retain a maximum of its own strategic nuclear power and has compelled the other party to give up more of its own, I cannot see much progress being made in the reduction of nuclear armaments." Also like Morgenthau, Kennan thought that some talks were better than no talks and that the SALT process was worth pursuing for that reason if for no other. He separated himself from Morgenthau on the issue of unilateral restraint. Kennan thought that unless the talks were "accompanied by *some* measures of unilateral restraint in weapons developments on the part of both parties," the talks would be meaningless. "A unilateral reduction of 10 percent [of nuclear weapons], immediately and as an act of good faith" was what Kennan had in mind.[89]

This suggestion of unilateral restraint was one of the first in a series of related proposals that Kennan put forth in the late 1970s and early 1980s. Although he flatly stated that "I am not suggesting any unilateral disarmament," the speeches and articles of his later years reveal his belief that when it came to arms control, perhaps the time had come for the superpowers to make some drastic, far-reaching changes.[90] As the only one of the few original postwar realists to survive into the century's final decade, Kennan made his presence felt by entering public debates on these issues with remarkable frequency.

Much of what Kennan had to say was not new. His crusade for a United States pledge of "no first use," for example, gained renewed attention when he coauthored a 1982 *Foreign Affairs* article on the subject with McGeorge Bundy, Robert McNamara, and Gerard C. Smith.[91] Kennan's advocacy of "no first use," however, dated back to his earliest writings on nuclear weapons. Kennan did come up with

89. George Kennan, *The Cloud of Danger: Current Realities of American Foreign Policy* (Boston, 1977), 203. Emphasis his.

90. See, for example, George Kennan, "On Nuclear War" (speech delivered on receipt of the Grenville Clark Prize, November 16, 1981) in Kennan, *Nuclear Delusion*, 194; and Kennan, "A Proposal for International Disarmament" (speech delivered on receipt of Albert Einstein Peace Prize, May 19, 1981), *ibid.*, 179.

91. George Kennan *et al.*, "Nuclear Weapons and the Atlantic Alliance," *Foreign Affairs*, LX (Spring, 1982), 753–68. See also Kennan *et al.*, "Back from the Brink," *Atlantic*, CCLVIII (August, 1986), 35–41.

117

some new ideas in the 1980s, including a proposal for the mutual reduction by 50 percent of the American and Soviet nuclear arsenals.[92] Kennan's ideas, both old and new, had one thing in common: they were widely discussed, bringing new energy to foreign policy debates.

Kennan's proposals nearly always were put forth with dramatic rhetorical style. His florid prose, heightened by his plaintive tone, made his appeals seem desperate. By the early 1980s, even farther out of the mainstream than he ever had been, Kennan was virtually a voice in the wilderness, largely ignored by official policy makers. Always given to hyperbole, he now brought it to new heights:

> I cannot help it. I hope I am not being unjust or uncharitable. But to me, in the light of these considerations, the readiness to use nuclear weapons against other human beings—against people whom we do not know, whom we have never seen, and whose guilt or innocence it is not for us to establish—and, in doing so, to place in jeopardy the natural structure upon which all civilization rests, as though the safety and the perceived interests of our generation were more important than everything that has ever taken place or could take place in civilization: this is nothing less than a presumption, a blasphemy, an indignity—an indignity of monstrous dimensions— offered to God.[93]

Such soaring rhetoric was not disingenuous; it was the product of Kennan's deeply held beliefs. After years of hope for the possibility of nuclear arms control, the frustration of failures in that area began to show. Kennan started to abandon the traditional realist belief in small steps and began to argue for a "bold and sweeping departure," a departure "that would cut surgically through the exaggerated anxieties, the self-engendered nightmares, and the sophisticated mathematics of destruction in which we have been entangled."[94]

Although Kennan was the most prolific and vociferous of the elderly realists, Morgenthau was similarly active in his later years. Until his death in 1980, Morgenthau's passionate pleas for new ways of

92. See Kennan, *Nuclear Delusion*, 175–82.
93. See George Kennan, "A Christian's View of the Arms Race," in Kennan, *Nuclear Delusion*, 201–207.
94. See Kennan, *Nuclear Delusion*, 179–80.

thinking on arms control echoed those of Kennan. Unlike Kennan, however, Morgenthau continued to advocate the "small steps" prescription. In one of his last writings, a short epilogue intended for a proposed reprint of *In Defense of the National Interest*, Morgenthau pointed to past successes in arms control as proof that progress could be achieved. The test ban treaty, the nonproliferation treaty, and the SALT agreements all "recognize implicitly," he wrote, "that the effects of nuclear armaments and nuclear war transcend the boundaries of any particular nation and that they are of concern, if not to humanity as a whole, at least to a multiplicity of nations." The "survival of civilization on this planet," he added, "is not a separate interest of the United States, the Soviet Union, France, Great Britain, India, Brazil, Argentina, and so forth, but it is an interest that transcends the limits of any of these individual nations [and] ties them together in a common, overarching interest."[95] The arms-control agreements in effect in 1980—limited as they were—were at least examples of nations coming together to address these "common, overarching" interests. In this, Morgenthau could take some limited satisfaction.

The real common ground between the United States, the Soviet Union, and other nuclear powers was fear. Even Acheson, the realist least sanguine about the merits of arms control, wrote that "we do have some common ground, the common ground of what Mr. Churchill has called mutual terror. Upon that and upon our own strength and courage it may be possible to bridge the chasm which yawns before us."[96] Along with the obvious fear of annihilation came increasing uneasiness about a financially ruinous arms race, concern for the environment, and fear that the complexity of new weapons systems could lead to unintended conflict through error.

The realists, like most people, saw arms-control agreements as a way of lessening the odds that disaster might strike. They knew, how-

95. Hans Morgenthau, "Epilogue," intended for 2nd ed. (1980) of Morgenthau, *In Defense of the National Interest: A Critical Examination of American Foreign Policy* (New York, 1951), copy of typescript in Box 112, Hans Morgenthau Papers, University of Virginia, Charlottesville.
96. Acheson, *Power and Diplomacy*, 39.

ever, that by itself an agreement could prevent nothing. It is hard to argue passionately for small steps, but that is precisely what the realists did. Only when small steps began to seem woefully inadequate did some of the realists make pleas for larger, more dramatic ones.

Ironically, it was Acheson, the least conciliatory of the realists, who best articulated the idea that where arms control was concerned, the national interest, the interest of other (sometimes rival) nations, and the global interest did not necessarily have to conflict. In 1951 he said: "We must deal with these [postwar] problems within a pattern of responsibility. . . . We must act with the consciousness that our responsibility is to interests broader than our own immediate American interests." Acheson's idea was that America must show that "we know today what Thomas Jefferson was talking about when he spoke of paying a decent respect to the opinions of mankind."[97] This was what should separate the United States from nations like the Soviet Union: that while the United States maintained the primacy of its own interests, it did not ignore the interests of others.

The realists recognized that the opinions of mankind and the opinions of the American people had a role to play in determining the distinction between usable and unusable force and, as a result, in delineating the responsible use of power. Just how much influence those opinions should have, however, was to be the topic of much and fierce debate.

97. Acheson quoted in McGeorge Bundy, ed., *The Pattern of Responsibility* (Boston, 1952), 297–98.

4 Democracy Versus Guardianship

> As concerns the great political decisions of the nuclear age, the technological expert does not know more than the man in the street or the politically responsible official.
>
> —*Hans Morgenthau, 1962*

Conducting foreign policy in the open and democratic society of the United States always has presented unique challenges. The division of power between the branches of government, the dominant influence of public opinion, and the presence of warring special interest groups all can make the pursuit of coherent and consistent foreign policies a difficult enterprise. Of course, these structural realities long have been recognized as sources of strength as well as of weakness, as redeeming attributes as well as congenital deficiencies. Alternating praise and lamentation over the American system of making and conducting foreign policy can be found in every period of the nation's history, and the postwar era has been no exception. There was among the realists some praise, but also considerable worry. The realists were concerned not only about the well-known effects of democracy on foreign policy, but also, to a lesser degree, about the effects of foreign policy decisions on democracy itself.

Usually, the galvanizing issue in the age-old debate over democracy versus guardianship has been *competence.* Beginning with Plato, political philosophers advocating guardianship have held that the people as a whole are incapable of knowing all that is required in order to rule wisely, and that given their limitations, they are better off entrusting the direction of the affairs of state to a chosen few. Governing, according to the advocates of guardianship, is best left to elites whose specialized training has prepared them for their roles as decision makers.

The issue of competence resonated anew in the postwar world, especially in regard to nuclear-weapons policies. New technology, new jargon, and complex military strategies gave rise to new speculation about the people's ability to pass judgment on complex issues and to rule themselves. The nuclear issue gave present-day "guardians" new grounds upon which to argue the need for elite leadership, and many of them made use of the opportunity. Guardians by nature, the realists, to a limited extent, also took up this cause.

In his comparatively recent *Controlling Nuclear Weapons* (1985), the political scientist Robert Dahl explored the question of whether the democratic process is "equipped to deal with questions of exceptional complexity." [1] Citing the problem of "specialized knowledge" as one of the most difficult for a democracy to overcome, Dahl pondered how and why a small group of people came to decide the most important issues facing the world, and he suggested the means by which those decisions might be put back into the hands of the general public. Dahl saw the problem as one of adaptation: the challenge was to find ways of adapting democratic institutions to a modern political world where secret information, technical knowledge, speed, and accuracy are at a premium.

For Americans in the 1980s, Dahl posed the same two questions that the realists had posed in the early postwar era. First, are the people capable of learning enough about the complex issues of national defense, diplomacy, and nuclear weapons to form reasonable, competent judgments on them? Second, is the democratic governance of these issues possible (and desirable) given the democratic process and its institutions as they exist in the United States?

Dahl's answer to both questions was yes (although he attached

1. Robert Dahl, *Controlling Nuclear Weapons: Democracy Versus Guardianship* (Syracuse, N.Y., 1985), 8.

some important qualifications to his second answer). He believed that although "instrumental elites" do have a special *technical* competence by virtue of their skills, they do not have any special *moral* competence or political vision. He found as much, if not more, moral competence among the people as in the elites. Dahl therefore saw a benefit in including more people in the policy-making process, and he focused on the need to increase the technical competence of the citizenry so that it could become an informed participant in political debates. For Dahl, this step depended on finding "new political institutions that would improve the political competence of both instrumental elites and citizens" so that a true partnership between them could be formed. Such a partnership necessarily would mean changing a system in which "for the better part of four decades" nuclear weapons policies had been debated, devised, and implemented by a small circle of elites "subject only weakly, if at all, to democratic procedures." [2]

The realists had different answers. They were not nearly as optimistic as Dahl about democracy, and they had little faith in the possibility of establishing widespread citizen competence. At bottom, they distrusted the citizenry in much the same way as had the eighteenth-century American Federalists. While the realists believed in democratic principles, they also felt that the wishes of the people had to be checked and balanced by the informed positions of the governing elite. Like the Federalists, they feared that a democracy not carefully balanced and directed could degenerate into mob rule. They believed that putting excessive power in the hands of the people could lead to factional disputes and paralysis even while, by the same token, it would leave society open to sudden, drastic change. In a nuclear world, they feared that excessive power in the hands of an aroused or angry citizenry could lead to more than political upheaval and revolution; it could lead to annihilation.

The realists wondered whether the citizenry was in fact educable on the issues of nuclear-weapons policies and postwar international politics. Actually, the question of the educability of the people had in-

2. *Ibid.*, 64, 33–34.

terested the realists long before the emergence of nuclear weapons brought it back into prominence. Lippmann, for example, had done some of his most influential social analysis on that subject, in writings dating as far back as the 1910s and 1920s. For the most part, Lippmann and the other realists (Niebuhr being a notable exception) continued over the years to lack Dahl's instinctive faith in the common man.

The realists' faith rested instead with the leaders, those who would form public opinion and provide direction for the people. Given the unfortunate realities of the modern political arena, where propaganda was ubiquitous and public opinion often was manipulated, the realists thought it vitally important for responsible leaders to step forward and offer the public enlightened, undistorted points of view. The realists maintained that democracy could work only if competent, informed leaders could gain the confidence of the people and lead them toward policies that would enhance the national interest.

Over time, however, the realists' faith in the capacity of leadership by a technical and political elite was shaken. Foreign-policy blunders, most notably the increasing military involvement in Vietnam, led the realists (and many other Americans) to question the wisdom of the so-called experts. The policies and events of the 1950s and 1960s left them to wonder whether the experts were in fact the best judges of the national interest. In general terms, the realists never abandoned their deep distrust of the people, public opinion, and mass rule; however, they did begin to question—sometimes unwittingly—whether traditional notions of guardianship provided solutions to the problems they saw in democracy.

The frustrations and dangers of the continuing arms race added to the realists' discomfort. Although they remained skeptical about the prospects for useful democratic participation in the formulation of nuclear-weapons policies, they came to the conclusion that the technical elite who had come to occupy America's "think tanks"—the elite that the historian Gregg Herken has called "the counsels of war" and that the journalist Fred Kaplan has called "the wizards of Armageddon"—had failed.[3] In something of a turnabout and in spite of their misgivings, the realists found themselves going back to the people. As with much of their other political commentary, the realists eventually adjusted their ideas about guardianship in a direction that was more consistent with democratic principles and traditional American tastes.

This adjustment made for much confusion and some contradiction, but that is not unusual among political philosophers discussing democracy and guardianship. Many a political theorist, within his own work, has exhibited conflicting ideas on the issue. The realists were, in some ways, elitists—sometimes blatantly so. All of them argued for one form of meritocracy or another, and most of their criticisms of democracy as it was practiced in the United States reflected a disdain for popular rule that approached aristocratic snobbery. Ultimately, however, the realists were able to retain some faith in the democratic process, and they sought to make that process more effective and relevant in the nuclear age. In that way, the fundamentally elitist realists prefigured the radically democratic Robert Dahl: like him, they sought to rescue the democratic process from death by suffocation. Except for Niebuhr, the realists never could muster the kind of faith in the average citizen that Dahl displayed, but like Dahl, they did come to believe that the common man possessed an amount of integrity, common sense, and moral competence that could not be ignored.

The Problem of Democracy

Some of the best and most entertaining writing by realists dealt directly with the "problem of democracy." It was a problem that elicited colorful descriptions and carefully crafted prescriptions. At its most basic level, the realists identified the problem as one of "drift." As the title of one of his earliest books, *Drift and Mastery* (1914), suggests, Lippmann long had been concerned about the possibility that the

3. Gregg Herken, *The Counsels of War* (New York, 1985). See also Fred Kaplan, *The Wizards of Armageddon* (New York, 1983).

United States might become "a rudderless nation" susceptible to the whims of public opinion. Lippmann feared that democracies were inherently undisciplined and prone to chronic, debilitating wanderings.

Lippmann's cure for drift was a counterbalance of strong leadership—and in government, that meant a strong executive branch.[4] This position became popular among the realists, for they feared drift almost as much as they feared excessive executive power. As Acheson pointed out in "The Responsibility for Decision in Foreign Policy" (1954), too much diffusion of political power could lead to chronic indecisiveness—a weakness no modern government could afford.[5] One thing Acheson had learned from his tenure in the executive branch was that the draining of power away from the executive could make the formation of sound policy difficult.

The problem of drift was magnified in the area of foreign affairs. All the realists, at one time or another, quoted Alexis de Tocqueville on the inferiority of democracies in regard to the conduct of foreign relations. They quoted passages such as the following, which highlights the inability of democracies to sustain delicate, prolonged diplomatic initiatives:

> I do not hesitate to say it is especially in the conduct of their foreign relations that democracies appear to me decidedly inferior to other governments. . . . Foreign politics demand scarcely any of those qualities which are peculiar to a democracy; they require, on the contrary, the perfect use of almost all those in which it is deficient. . . . [A] democracy can only with a great deal of difficulty regulate the details of an important undertaking, persevere in a fixed design, and work out its execution in spite of serious obstacles. It cannot combine its measures with secrecy or await their consequences with patience. These are qualities which more especially belong to an individual or an aristocracy.[6]

4. See, for example, Walter Lippmann, *Essays in the Public Philosophy*, (Boston, 1955), *passim*.

5. Dean Acheson, "The Responsibility for Decision in Foreign Policy," *Yale Review*, XLIV (September, 1954), 1–12.

6. Tocqueville quoted in Dean Acheson, *A Citizen Looks at Congress* (New York, 1957), 86–87.

Those at the helm of a democracy did not have all of the instruments they needed to be successful in foreign relations—at least, they were at a distinct disadvantage compared with autocrats or oligarchs. They had to fight drift with what they had, which was not very much at all.

"The question," as Acheson put it after considering Tocqueville's perceptive criticism, "is whether the checking and balancing pre-scribed by the Constitution is so conducted as to permit a continuity of policy, involving over a period of years the maintenance of distasteful measures."[7] Even though distasteful measures rarely had the enthu-siastic support of the people, the government had to have the power to use them. Acheson and others worried about the system's built-in tendency toward vacillation and the relative ease with which the path of least resistance could be taken. The realists believed that there were times when the people had to be told to swallow the medicine, no mat-ter how bad it tasted.

These observations led the realists to conclude that there were cer-tain varieties of foreign policy that were ill suited for the United States. Distasteful measures could be employed, and sustained commitments could be made, but only at great cost. There was a bottom to the res-ervoir of consensus that could be maintained; there was a short limit to the patience of the people. Lippmann explained this phenomenon in *The Cold War,* his response to Kennan's "X" article. Lippmann's analysis featured the argument that the policy of containment outlined by Kennan played into America's weaknesses rather than its strengths.

Lippmann criticized Kennan's idea of containment because, among other reasons, it was based on a policy of "patient persistence." Neither patience nor persistence was often seen in American foreign policy in the past, nor were these qualities likely to be seen in the future. Ken-nan's call for the commitment of "unalterable counterforce" at every point where the Soviets showed signs of encroachment was, in essence, a policy of holding the line, a wearing down of the opponent through constant vigilance.[8] But if the United States were to be able to react

7. *Ibid.,* 35.
8. Walter Lippmann, *The Cold War: A Study in U.S. Foreign Policy* (Boston, 1947), 13–15.

with a show of strength at what Kennan called "a series of constantly shifting geographical and political points," it would need sustained economic and political support from the American people. Lippmann thought that some such support could be gathered, but how long it could be maintained was in doubt. He urged that the concept of containment be refined and pared down to cover only the nation's most vital interests.

"How," asked Lippmann, "under the Constitution of the United States, is Mr. X going to work out an arrangement by which the Department of State has the money and military power always available in sufficient amounts to apply 'counterforce' at constantly shifting points all over the world?" The answer, Lippmann knew, was that Mr. X could not work out any such thing. Neither the State Department nor any other arm of the government could embark on a long-range, ill-defined, amorphous policy such as containment with any reasonable chance of success. Americans, Lippmann was convinced, had short attention spans and needed quick dividends to justify their investments. Because of this, he felt certain that Mr. X's policy would backfire. "The Americans," he concluded, "would themselves be frustrated by Mr. X's policy before the Russians were." [9]

Ironically, Kennan's assessment of American democracy and its relationship to foreign policy was strikingly similar to Lippmann's. In fact, Kennan immediately recognized the insight of his critic and later granted that Lippmann had pointed out the major shortcomings of containment as it had been sketched in the "X" article. Kennan, in a description that mirrored Lippmann's point of view, likened the American democracy to a dimwitted but dangerous beast. In a 1950 lecture later included in his book *American Diplomacy*, Kennan compared the American democracy to "one of those prehistoric monsters with a body as long as [a] room and a brain the size of a pin." This monster, he explained, "lies there in his comfortable primeval mud and pays little attention to his environment; he is slow to wrath—in fact, you practically have to whack his tail off to make him aware that his interests are

9. *Ibid.*, 20.

being disturbed; but, once he grasps this, he lays about him with such blind determination that he not only destroys his adversary but largely wrecks his native habitat."[10] All brawn and no brains, Kennan concluded, a democracy has fearsome strength, but a pitiful lack of coordination.

Kennan later became more specific in his criticism, citing both Congress and the weight of public opinion as the sources of democracy's ineptitude. Congress, Kennan argued, can act upon foreign policy "only fitfully, in great ponderous lurches."[11] It can establish direction and set limits, but it cannot carry out policies that require even a modest amount of dexterity. Similarly, Kennan considered public opinion to be useful for establishing direction and setting limits over the long term; over the short term, it tended to be a liability. "I think the record indicates," argued Kennan in 1950, "that in the short term our public opinion, or what passes for public opinion in official Washington, can be easily led astray into areas of emotionalism and subjectivity which make a poor and inadequate guide for public action."[12] Kennan agreed with the conclusion Lippmann reached in 1925 that "the force of public opinion" is "partisan" and "spasmodic," and therefore of dubious value to policy makers.[13]

These observations led Kennan to conclude that the United States, because of the very nature of its government, was severely limited as to what it could accomplish in foreign affairs. In his *Memoirs* he asked himself "whether a government so constituted should deceive itself into believing that it is capable of conducting a mature, consistent, and discriminating foreign policy." He concluded that "increasingly, with the years, my answer would tend to be in the negative."[14] This rationale

10. George Kennan, *American Diplomacy* (Rev. ed.; Chicago, 1984), 66.
11. George Kennan, *The Cloud of Danger: Current Realities of American Foreign Policy* (Boston, 1977), 6.
12. Kennan, *American Diplomacy*, 93.
13. Walter Lippmann, *The Phantom Public: A Sequel to "Public Opinion"* (New York, 1927), 151.
14. George Kennan, *Memoirs, 1925–1950* (Boston, 1967), 295, Vol. I of Kennan, *Memoirs*, 2 vols.

later would serve to justify his own self-proclaimed proclivity toward a new isolationism; the United States, in his opinion, was not politically equipped for certain kinds of activism overseas.[15] When it came to devising and implementing complex policies, democracy's vices outweighed its virtues: the nation vacillated between lethargy and hyperactivity, and there was no apparent way to regulate its behavior.

The realists had lived through a cycle of fearsome convulsions that they hoped would not be repeated. They had witnessed the effects of an aroused democracy during the two world wars, and they had lived with the consequences of a stagnating, drifting democracy both in the interwar years and in the 1950s. They had found both the aroused and the stagnated postures to be equally unsatisfactory. When aroused, democracies tended toward extremism, acting in anger and with vengeance. Such arousal led to vindictive policies such as area bombing and unconditional surrender. When stagnated, democracies drifted aimlessly, occasionally toward a precipice. The appeasement debacle of the late 1930s and the stranglehold of the military-industrial complex in the 1950s were examples of what could happen to societies paralyzed by internal constraints. Accepting the fact that the basic elements of the system could not be changed, the realists searched for ways to work with that system to make it more manageable and therefore more purposeful.

Lippmann never stopped pointing out the flaws in democracy, even while simultaneously seeking ways to make democratic rule more consistent with the pursuit of the national interest. The dilemma, as he saw it, was that "the problems that vex democracy seem to be unmanageable by democratic methods." Democracies, he observed, seemed "unable to find solutions of their greatest problems except through centralized governing by means of extensive rules which necessarily ignore the principle of assent."[16] He warned against investing the principle of majority rule with "mystical significance." Majority rule was a useful "political device," he argued, but it did not signal absolute truth

15. See Kennan interview with George Urban, in George Kennan, *Encounters with Kennan: The Great Debate*, ed. Daniel Moynihan (London, 1979), esp. 18–19.

16. Lippmann, *Phantom Public*, 189–90.

or ultimate wisdom. The mere fact that 51 percent of the people believed something to be right did not necessarily make it so. The determination of right and wrong—or of the proper path to pursuing the national interest—should not, Lippmann reiterated, rest solely on the results of a poll of the people. As one Lippmann scholar, Charles Wellborn, has put it, Lippmann doubted "the caliber of wisdom arising from the majority." [17]

Lippmann's distrust of majority rule grew out of his belief that norms should not be subject to the changing winds of each new day. Relatively stable norms were deeply rooted in the traditions of Western civilization and offered a sturdy, unyielding foundation for the "public philosophy." It remained for the leaders of each generation to articulate that philosophy and make it relevant to daily affairs. Yet Lippmann thought that the leaders failed more than they succeeded; in fact, he saw the history of the liberal democracies in the twentieth century as a history of failure to understand the dangers of unbridled majoritarian rule. The rise of the Nazis, for example, illustrated what could happen when political frustration, economic hardship, and propaganda converged. In Germany in the 1930s the majority ruled, but eventually the results were devastating. The same could be said of postwar America. When someone like Senator Joseph McCarthy could win the support of a large segment of the population with his demagoguery—for however limited a time—it brought into serious question the usefulness of majority rule. The problem was that special interests and demagoguery too often were mistaken for the national interest.

Lippmann knew all too well the havoc that propaganda could wreak upon the political process, and he concluded that voters faced serious obstacles in gathering truthful information. The media distorted facts, roused the people with inflammatory rhetoric, and promoted special interests. It was exceedingly difficult, if not impossible, for voters to be disinterested, to remain above the partisan frays in pursuit of the na-

17. See Walter Lippmann, "Why Should the Majority Rule?" *Harper's*, CLII (March, 1926), 399–405. For commentary on this aspect of Lippmann's thought, see Charles Wellborn, *Twentieth Century Pilgrimage: Walter Lippmann and the Public Philosophy* (Baton Rouge, 1969), 73–74.

tional interest. This did not disqualify the people from playing a role in the political process, but it did, Lippmann believed, place limits on the amount of weight that should be given to their opinion as it was expressed at any given time.

Lippmann made a significant distinction between The People and *The People:* The People were citizens of a specific time and place— citizens who expressed the interests of a living population. *The People* were a historic community that represented civilization itself; they were the connected generations of the living, the dead, and those yet to be born.[18] Unfortunately, The People rarely measured up to their historic role, leaving it up to others to assume responsibility for the wider interests of *The People.*

In fact, that task fell to the executive and to a few nongovernmental leaders who could speak for the larger interests of the nation. Morgenthau saw the situation as one where the statesman must "take the long view," and persuade the people who want "quick results" that they are being shortsighted. Those who are willing to "sacrifice tomorrow's real benefit for today's apparent advantage" must be corrected by forceful leaders with vision.[19] Those who are prone to forget the past also must be chastised. But educating the public, the realists found, was an arduous task. Not only was there a sense of complacency in the postwar public, but there also appeared to be complacency in the nation's leadership.

The realists maintained that the public and its leaders had to interact: one had to criticize the other, each had to energize its counterpart. This dynamic, as the Federalists had pointed out, would prohibit a tyranny of the majority or, conversely, a tyranny of the executive or some other group of powerful interests. In the long run, open criticism and opposition would form a stabilizing force, rescuing arrogant leaders from their own delusions and protecting the voters from their own impulsive tendencies. This was nothing new—the theory, as has been pointed out, was as old as the Republic; what *was* new, as the realists

18. Lippmann, *Public Philosophy,* 33–36.
19. Hans Morgenthau, *In Defense of the National Interest: A Critical Examination of American Foreign Policy* (New York, 1951), 223.

saw it, was that the system was now in dire need of an infusion of energy. Both sides were breaking down, and there was little useful criticism coming from either camp. Dynamism had given way to stagnation, and the crisis of competence had deepened.

This decline called for a modernizing of democratic theory and democratic governance. Something had to be done if the public was ever to become a responsible partner in the policy-making process in the nuclear age. The realists still accepted ideas such as the one embodied in Niebuhr's much-quoted aphorism, "Man's capacity for justice makes democracy possible; but man's inclination to injustice makes democracy necessary." For democracy to have any effect in the postwar world, however, the role of the people had to be reconsidered.[20] America's rise to globalism had presented the nation with a variety of complex issues to decide, the most important of which was how to use (or not use) atomic weapons. Given their past doubts about the common man's judgment, the realists could not help but be uneasy about the role of the public in determining more complicated future policy. If the public had been so unsuccessful before, what would the future bring?

The realists' worries of the postwar era were based on the same misgivings they had held previously, but atomic weapons made things seem worse. As early as 1914, Lippmann noted that one of the great problems of the modern age was that political change was not keeping pace with technological change.[21] During World War II, Lippmann sensed that as the world changed irrevocably, the American voting public remained essentially the same, a creature of its old habits. As in the past, people had limited time to study issues, and they formed their opinions on even the most complex issues based on the little they had read in the newspaper or heard on the radio.[22] The voting public ap-

20. Reinhold Niebuhr, *The Children of Light and the Children of Darkness: A Vindication of Democracy and a Critique of Its Traditional Defense* (New York, 1944), ix.

21. See Walter Lippmann, *Drift and Mastery: An Attempt to Diagnose the Current Unrest* (New York, 1914), chap. 8.

22. Walter Lippmann, "Everybody's Business and Nobody's," ("Today and Tomorrow," April 10, 1941), in Walter Lippmann Papers, Yale University, New Haven.

peared to be ill equipped to meet the challenges of postwar politics; the issues simply could not be addressed in the cursory manner to which most people had grown accustomed.

Whereas the constraints of time and competence previously had had only relatively minor impact, they threatened to have major consequences in the future. There were many complex issues to consider and comparatively few people possessing the time, technical knowledge, and inclination to engage themselves in the debates. The realists believed that leaders would have to undertake new initiatives to educate the public. Otherwise, the public, in its ignorance, would not be able to participate in policy debates in a constructive way.

"The environment is complex," wrote Lippmann in 1925. "Man's political capacity is simple. Can a bridge be built between them?" As this query took on a new urgency, the realists offered some suggestions, all of which were consistent with their previous critiques of democracy. As Niebuhr put it, "At a time when technological society requires technological competence as well as moral good will, modern democracies are more dependent than ever upon competent elites— particularly, as we have noted, in the determination of foreign policy." Yet in Niebuhr's view these elites had a specific purpose: to serve as the bridge for which Lippmann was searching, the bridge between man's simple political capacity and the complex environment. "The people cannot give their leaders absolute trust," Niebuhr explained; "policies must be subject to periodic review and possible veto." [23]

The existence of competent elites to serve as bridges or translators for the public so that they could gain access to and understand the issues of the day did not absolve the citizenry of the duty to involve themselves in the political process. Addressing the problem of "the unavoidable gap between specialized knowledge and public understanding" in his foreword to *Russia, the Atom, and the West* (1957), Kennan wrote, "I am reluctant to cross that crucial border beyond which one admits that foreign affairs are exclusively the province of the full-time

23. Reinhold Niebuhr, "Democracy's Foreign Policy Dilemma," *New Leader,* XLIV (October 2, 1961), 22–23.

professional, in which the views of the private citizen can have no value." He concluded that "for the moment, at least, the citizen must still try to think, to have opinions, and to express them when there are those who would like to listen."[24] The competent elites were not so infallibly competent as no longer to need the criticism of the thinking citizen.

Citizens also had a duty to make sure that the competent elites remained accountable to the people for the policies that those elites recommended and implemented. Unfortunately, the citizens were not always able to fulfill that obligation. There was great fear among the realists that the elites were forming a circle that existed outside of democratic control. The most obvious manifestation of this phenomenon was the military-industrial complex, wherein private corporations and government agencies combined to run America's defense establishment. Military planning and procurement carried out by small groups of politically and economically powerful men created vested interests and bureaucratic alliances that were insulated from the democratic process. Morgenthau called this development the "new feudalism," implying that this concentration of private wealth and power, tacitly backed by the government bureaucracy, had circumvented and then overrun the power of the state and the power of the individual.[25]

The realists speculated on ways to overcome the new feudalism and crack its thickly insulated shell. The question was how to infuse democracy into the system without harming the national interest or causing any undue strife. It was a question they never completely answered, but they did conclude that through education and participation in the political process, the people could make their presence felt: by making their opinions known, the people could establish the parameters of acceptable policies, policies that in turn would be put in final form and implemented by the elites.

The realists also saw the limits of their own prescription. The voice

24. George Kennan, *Russia, the Atom, and the West* (New York, 1957), vii.

25. See Hans Morgenthau, "The New Despotism and the New Feudalism," typescript in Box 99, Hans Morgenthau Papers, University of Virginia, Charlottesville. See also Kennan, *Cloud of Danger*, 12–14.

of the people could account for only one part of the political process. When the people got carried away, they were nearly always counterproductive. The realists saw the student radicalism of the 1960s as the perfect illustration of overcompensation for the new feudalism. At its peak, the unrest served only to confirm their worst fears about democracy.

Kennan castigated the New Left and the student radicals allied with it in a widely noted 1968 speech that was printed in the *New York Times Magazine*. Originally prepared as an address to be delivered at Swarthmore College, the speech attracted so much attention after its appearance in the newspaper that it later was reprinted in book form along with reactions from students and others, as well as a rejoinder by Kennan.[26] *Democracy and the Student Left* (1968) separated Kennan from the other realists by its harshness of tone and severity of judgment; nevertheless, it revealed many realist anxieties. Even Morgenthau, who won the praise of many New Left devotees for his opposition to the war in Vietnam, could not have been pleased by the actions of the extremists Kennan referred to as "the angry ones." All of the realists feared unrestrained popular agitation, although some were more accepting than others of the students' attempt to participate in the political process. Kennan, however, was offended by the "unreflective," "impatient," and "overstimulated" student radicals.

What Kennan objected to most was the students' lack of historical perspective, their lack of respect for the governmental structure, and their tactics for combating the status quo. He found their ideas about participatory democracy—"the notion that ordinary people should be able to affect all decisions that control their lives"—to be misguided. "Does anyone seriously believe that the process of government could effectively work this way?" he asked. "It is not that there is no place in our political life for the challenging and stimulating influence of an idealistic, progressive, and determined minority," he explained, "but there is no place for it as a purely critical, irresponsible, and politically

26. George Kennan, "Rebels Without a Program," *New York Times Magazine* (January 21, 1968), 22–23, 60–61, 69–71; Kennan, *Democracy and the Student Left* (Boston, 1968).

unorganized force, attempting to act directly on an Executive for which it has no respect and sees no alternative." [27] To Kennan, the students seemed arrogant: they expected their grievances to be addressed immediately and directly. He concluded that this was no way for a great power to conduct its foreign affairs; the nation could not be driven by such pressures.

Kennan advised the students to seek redress through the polls: that was the honorable, constructive, and responsible thing to do. Turning the example of Henry David Thoreau around on the radicals, for many of whom *Civil Disobedience* had been an inspiration, Kennan described the master of Walden as a political and philosophical failure who had been "anarchical" in his protests against the Mexican War and slavery. Kennan criticized Thoreau for taking "refuge in the concept of direct action by the people" and called his gesture of spending time in the Concord jail a "claim to moral superiority." Kennan's sympathies were with abolitionist reformers who chose to eschew the open defiance of firebrands like Thoreau. Such practical, thoughtful abolitionists, argued Kennan, were more successful than Thoreau; they participated in the democratic process without insisting on "direct action by the people." These abolitionists worked to cajole and persuade, and eventually they were successful.

The student radicals, all the realists agreed, went too far. Even so, their actions were a reminder that the American democracy needed continuous readjustment. In 1965, Lippmann wrote a column that summarized the realists' view of the student radicals and of the state of democracy in contemporary America. Calling the student demonstrations "self-defeating," Lippmann added that "they are, it seems to me, a pathetic reminder of what happens in a free country when responsible debate on great matters of life and death is throttled down and discouraged." The problem, again, was education and leadership. The public had to be informed on the issues, and it had to be listened to when it reached a verdict. But this combination, Lippmann noted, called for leadership that was willing to both guide and listen.

27. Kennan, *Democracy and the Student Left,* 210–11.

"There is only one way a democratic people can be won over and convinced," Lippmann concluded in his article, "and that is by enabling the people to hear informed debate by its responsible leaders." When "debate by those who have a right to know is discouraged," he argued, "there is no responsible guidance of public opinion." Without responsible guidance, the people were merely an unchanneled force in search of an outlet. "Given the situation," Lippmann wrote, "we must not be surprised that these great matters are then taken to the teach-ins and out into the streets."[28]

The greatest problems that democracy faced were its volatility, its susceptibility to being dominated by powerful interests, and the requirement of competence. The democratic system was, as the realists saw it, a precariously balanced house of cards. Literally hundreds of hazards could cause its collapse. Excessive activism and its opposite, stagnation, were only two of the more visible of these hazards. The realists' most pressing fear in the nuclear age, however, concerned the issues of knowledge and competence. The realists wondered how the house of cards could continue to stand when the very future of meaningful democratic debate was in doubt owing to the complexity of the issues.

The Role of the Guardians

Student radicalism was merely one manifestation of what could go wrong with democracy. It illustrated to the realists what could happen when one segment of the population gathered strength and momentum of its own outside the normal channels of political debate. In the realists' view, public opinion needed guidance, which in turn required disinterested leaders. Such leaders on occasion could even be partisan, so long as they fulfilled their essential purpose of keeping the nation on a steady course. These leaders—or guardians—would provide vision and perspective. They also would be called upon to teach.

"Once [public men] refuse to lead opinion and prefer to be led by

28. Walter Lippmann, "On the Student Demonstrations" ("Today and Tomorrow," October 26, 1965), in Lippmann Papers.

it," wrote Lippmann in 1925, "they make impossible the formation of sound public opinion." In essence, the role of the guardians was to make, or at least direct, public opinion, not follow it. "Effective government," he suggested, "cannot be conducted by legislators and officials who, when a question is presented, ask themselves first and last not what is the truth and what is the right and necessary course but 'what does the Gallup poll say?' and 'how do the editors and commentators line up?' "[29] According to the realists, any leader who treated the public opinion poll as "an oracle" was not really a leader—and certainly not a guardian—at all.[30]

The principal leader and chief guardian of the American nation and its national interest was the president. "It is for the president," wrote Morgenthau in 1949, "to reassert his historic role as both the initiator of policy and the awakener of public opinion." Morgenthau likened American public opinion to a "slumbering giant" that needed prodding and direction from above.[31] Most of the realists held Theodore Roosevelt to be the premier example of the kind of presidential leadership that was needed in the twentieth century. They admired Roosevelt's magnetism, vigor, and ability to mobilize the people behind his initiatives.[32]

In the mid-1950s, Acheson proposed that time had brought about "a reversal of the legislative and executive roles as outlined in the Constitution." As Acheson saw it, "Today—and even more tomorrow—it is the President who initiates and proposes policy; it is the Congress which approves, modifies, or vetoes."[33] Acheson saw this as a positive development. The president was now freer to set the agenda, and more often than not, Congress was forced to react to it. This change was brought about in part by the effects of the technological and informa-

29. Lippmann, "Everybody's Business and Nobody's."
30. Morgenthau used the word *oracle* in reference to public opinion polls in Hans Morgenthau, *The Purpose of American Politics* (New York, 1960), 262–63.
31. Hans Morgenthau, "The Conduct of American Foreign Policy," *Parliamentary Affairs*, III (Winter, 1949), 161.
32. See, for example, Acheson, "Responsibility for Decision in Foreign Policy."
33. Acheson, *A Citizen Looks at Congress*, 117.

tional revolutions of the twentieth century. With so much information to sift through and absorb, leaders first had to make certain that laymen had access to the information they needed. Once that was achieved, the leaders had to insure that the public was able to make sense of that information. The president, according to Acheson, was the primary leader; Congress played a supporting role.

The president's role was critical because only he had complete access to all national security information and only he saw the complete picture of what was happening in the world. The executive branch had the primary responsibility for seeing that the public was informed on the most vital issues of the day and that such issues were explained in language that could be understood. The president had advisers and specialists to aid him in his understanding of the most complex issues, and it was the president's duty to pass his understanding along to his constituents. "The greatest leaders," said Lippmann, "are also the greatest teachers."

As teacher and translator, the president wielded immense influence. His role was that of mediator between the experts and the people. How he framed the problems facing the country and how he explained proposed solutions to those problems would have a great effect on the formation of public opinion. As Lippmann put it, only the president was in a position to "keep the country well informed without destroying the privacy which is essential to diplomatic negotiations" or jeopardizing national security secrets. This task of informing the public was best accomplished "by periodic talks, one might almost say lectures, given by the President or Secretary of State explaining the situation and how it got to be what it is, and what are the difficulties and issues which have to be dealt with." [34] In this way, the executive branch could provide a cure for some of the ills of democracy. It could safeguard secrets, conduct sensitive negotiations, and provide leadership by doing what it thought to be proper. It could do all of this, however, only if it continually explained to the public the rationale behind its policies.

34. Walter Lippmann, "Rusk on Quiet Diplomacy" ("Today and Tomorrow," January 26, 1961), in Lippmann Papers.

On the other hand, Lippmann ridiculed those who would open every matter to public inspection. He maintained that such exhaustive debate was neither practical nor conducive to good government. In 1949 Lippmann made the following unfavorable comparison: "The effort of laymen who know virtually nothing about nuclear physics, to determine what is a secret and how to guard it, is rather like what would happen if, say, Senator Hickenlooper woke up one morning and found he had been appointed the censor of the Chinese nationalist press. I hope I do him no injustice in assuming that his ability to read Chinese is no greater than his knowledge of the science of nuclear physics."[35] Lippmann argued that when too many unskilled and uninformed people, including congressmen, tried to direct policy in areas they knew little about, it was difficult for government to operate effectively. Laymen—policy makers included—had to find and rely on trusted specialists, not charlatans who had an opinion on everything, even on things they did not understand.

The question of the proper role for Congress drew considerable attention. Even though Congress was the object of a moderate amount of derision on the part of the realists, most of them agreed that it, too, could serve as a guardian. Acheson had some specific ideas, in the main recommending a consulting role for Congress. "The principal activity for Congress today," wrote Acheson in 1957, "is investigation in all its branches." He cited as potentially "useful" the special committee, "with counsel, sleuths, publicity agents, radio and television, and two hundred or more standing committees and joint committees charged with constant supervision of the executive agencies." Congress "cannot initiate," he argued, "it cannot create." But "it can test and criticize and might well brand the meretricious as such before it has had a chance to do much harm."[36]

Acheson hoped that Congress would advise, consent, and educate. He believed that congressional committees could be effective in laying the groundwork for informed public debate. The task of such commit-

35. Walter Lippmann, "Senators, Scientists, and Secrecy" ("Today and Tomorrow," May 23, 1949), in Lippmann Papers.
36. Acheson, *A Citizen Looks at Congress*, 118–19.

141

tees, he wrote, was "to obtain a solid foundation for judgment" on policies being considered. He cited the Subcommittee on the Air Force of the Senate Armed Services Committee of the Eighty-fourth Congress as an excellent example of the positive work that Congress could do. Under the leadership of Senator Stuart Symington—and generally known as the Symington committee—the subcommittee undertook a comprehensive evaluation of the air force's needs and demands, and informed the public on many complex and important defense issues.[37] By uncovering, examining, and chronicling these issues, Congress was performing a limited but vital guardianship function.

Acheson was well aware, however, that Congress could forget its limited role and try to steal the limelight. Congress had to be checked by a strong executive branch; otherwise, the resulting power imbalance would make proper guardianship impossible. Acheson and most other realists complained incessantly about the tendency of Congress to get out of control and lose its discipline. Acheson was annoyed, for example, that one sixth of his working days in Washington were devoted to preparing for and attending congressional meetings. This was a clear example, he felt, of Congress overreaching its function.[38] The realists were willing to tolerate a certain amount of friction between Congress and the executive; they recognized that such friction was what made the system work. What they would not tolerate was a system where the executive was stalemated by a grandstanding Congress, or where Congress was entirely circumvented by an overly independent executive.

While the realists accepted the fact that the pendulum of influence swung back and forth between the executive and the legislative branches, they continued to argue that both branches had guardianship duties. The duties of each were determined by the actions of the other. Morgenthau pointed to changes in emphasis in his own writing as evidence that he did not consider guardianship to be a fixed assignment. In 1969 he remembered how he "used to implore a succession

37. *Ibid.*, 97–99.
38. Dean Acheson, "Legislative-Executive Relations," *Yale Review*, XLV (June, 1956), 485.

of Presidents to reassert their Constitutional powers against Congress"; later, in the wake of the Eisenhower-Dulles foreign policies, he "urged the Senate Foreign Relations Committee to establish itself as a kind of counter-Department of State." Then, "from 1965 onwards," he recalled, he had "welcomed the influence that Congress, the Senate, or for that matter, any other agency of government" exerted in attempts to change the course of American foreign policy.[39]

There were numerous reasons why guardianship failed on the executive and legislative levels; the important thing was to make certain that both branches did not fail simultaneously. Morgenthau, for one, was willing to lend support to either side, depending on which needed bolstering. Most realists were less willing than Morgenthau to support increases in legislative power, but most at least understood his increasing frustration with the executive branch. The realists generally agreed with Morgenthau's complaint that the electoral process had been reduced to almost meaningless choices between "Tweedledee and Tweedledum," and they considered that political corruption had alienated the people from the political process. By the early 1970s, Morgenthau was arguing that America needed "a new faith carried by social forces that will create new political institutions and procedures commensurate with new tasks."[40] Although his frustrations were not greatly different from those of the student radicals, his proposals for change were far less drastic. Morgenthau, unlike the radicals, believed that constructive change could not be achieved without the help of guardians.

Since the need for guardians was well established among the realists, the final question concerned who those guardians would be. Niebuhr referred to the guardians as an aristocracy. "The health of a democracy," he claimed, "requires a fluid, and, if possible, multiple aristocracy, consisting of [persons] who select themselves and are selected by their interest in and ability to understand the many facets of

39. Hans Morgenthau, "Congress and Foreign Policy," *New Republic*, CLX (June 14, 1969), 17.

40. Hans Morgenthau, "The Decline of Democratic Government," *New Republic*, CLXXI (November 9, 1974), 18.

foreign policy." Perhaps *aristocracy* was "the wrong word for designating a select group or groups in a community which have competence above the average public," he went on to say, but "ideally, a free society creates various aristocracies or elite groups in various fields of culture and political affairs." In any case, the important point was that these "aristocracies" had to remain open and constantly changing. Admission to them was to be based on knowledge and ability, not social class.[41]

Niebuhr's aristocracy of competence was similar to but less clearly defined than Kennan's proposals. Frustrated with the paralysis he perceived in the system, Kennan in his later years began to contemplate structural reform. By the mid-1970s, he was proposing the creation of a group of five hundred to a thousand people to serve as a pool of potential officeholders. Appointment to the group, he wrote, "would be by some detached and austere authority such as the Supreme Court, and membership in it would represent recognition of distinction in our national life achieved by a man's own efforts outside the field of political competition." The idea was that institutional reforms had to be made to insure that office seekers were "selected from among the better men in our country, and not from among the vulgar, dull, sluggish, and untutored."[42]

Like Niebuhr, Kennan was not talking about an inherited aristocracy, but a meritocracy. To be counted among the elite and to become a guardian, one had to earn that position, preferably through excellence in a field outside of politics. Kennan hoped that these meritorious guardians would not tolerate the mediocre policies, based on appeals to the lowest common denominator, that professional politicians frequently peddled. The elite would insist upon excellence and thereby would gain the confidence of the public in their leadership. Kennan became convinced that what the country needed was a talented minority that was capable of leadership. Such a group would be equipped (and positioned) to lead rather than follow public opinion.

41. Reinhold Niebuhr, "The Democratic Elite and American Foreign Policy," in *Walter Lippmann and His Times,* ed. Marquis Childs (New York, 1959), 170–75.
42. Kennan, *Encounters with Kennan,* 28–29.

This was not just a passing fancy. Kennan later revised and updated his idea of a council of the elite. In his introduction to Norman Cousins' *Pathology of Power* (1987), Kennan reiterated his desire to see an elite group of some kind established. This time, however, Kennan suggested that an advisory board to the president, rather than a pool of potential officeholders, be established out of such a group. Instead of being candidates for elective office themselves, the members of this council would be wise men—"a body of men and women (and not too many of them) made wise by natural aptitude and long experience in the ways of the world, people wholly disengaged (or at least in the late stages of their careers) from the political process, people enjoying sufficient public respect and confidence so that their views would carry weight." The council's main task would be to "offer thoughtful and measured advice in the great matters of war and peace" to the president, advice that he "is unlikely to get from the men normally around him in the turmoil of his office."[43] This whole description, it should be noted, sounded suspiciously like self-description: given the requirements put forward, Kennan himself would have been the ideal person to sit on such a council.

Whether the goal was to create a screening device for candidates or a purely advisory body, Kennan's call for an elite council was to a certain extent undemocratic. His suggestion did contain, however, a democratic component that should not be overlooked. Kennan's council was to be formed for the express purpose of educating the president and the public as to the consequences of various policies. It was to wake the government and the people out of their slumber in regard to the arms race, and it was to offer new ideas to counteract and combat inertia. It was, in effect, to give power to the people (and their government) by offering leadership in a different direction. Unencumbered by the exigencies of domestic politics and the pressures exerted by special interests and bureaucracies, the council would be free to offer suggestions for bold and sweeping reforms, as well as advice on contro-

43. George Kennan, introduction to Norman Cousins, *The Pathology of Power* (New York, 1987).

145

versial policies. It would have no binding authority, only the power of ideas that the people would accept or reject on their own.

The arms race, Kennan concluded, had been pursued unquestioningly, "almost involuntarily." Americans had embarked upon it, he sighed, "like the victims of some sort of hypnotism, like men in a dream, like lemmings headed for the sea, like the children of Hamlin marching blindly along behind the Pied Piper." [44] Kennan and the other realists hoped that the guardians could jolt the people and the government out of this mesmerized state. Whether the guardians in fact had any special vision was open to debate; there was much to suggest that they might not. But the realists all agreed that whatever liabilities the guardians might have, they also had special talents that ought to be tapped.

Where Scientific Knowledge and Political Judgment Meet: The Need for Democratic Review

Despite all their arguments concerning the need for guardians and experts, particularly in the nuclear age, the realists never abandoned the fundamental belief in the need for democratic review. Their complaints about the weaknesses and inefficiencies of democracy were genuine, and their frustrations and misgivings were deeply felt, but in the end they acknowledged that the people must have the final say. Even Kennan, the realist most distrusting of the people, eventually found himself going back to them for support of his disarmament proposals.

Kennan's turn to the public in his later years was more than a case of strange bedfellows, it symbolized the realists' ambivalence on the question of guardianship. In 1981, Kennan called the growing antinuclear movement in the United States and Europe "the most striking phenomenon of the beginning of the 1980s." He added approvingly

44. George Kennan, "A Proposal for International Disarmament" (speech delivered on receipt of the Albert Einstein Peace Price, May 19, 1981), in Kennan, *The Nuclear Delusion: Soviet-American Relations in the Atomic Age* (New York, 1982), 176.

that it was so "impressive" that governments would have no choice but to contend with it. "This movement," he observed, "is too powerful, too elementary, too deeply embedded in the natural human instinct for self-preservation, to be brushed aside." [45] In endorsing this grass-roots movement, Kennan fulfilled his role as a guardian seeking to shape public opinion. He was still an elitist, but he had become an elitist who recognized that guardianship could not exist apart from the consent of the governed. Policies emanating from disconnected guardians would have no moral standing and little chance for popular support.

In a particularly enlightening profile of Kennan, the historian and journalist Ronald Steel suggested that Kennan's antinuclear crusade was fueled in part by the realization that the public possesses powers of discernment that have for too long been discounted. Kennan's later work, Steel argued, was addressed to the public, not the experts; indeed, Kennan "helped rouse a wider public to the most momentous, and perhaps the final issue of our time." [46] In doing this, Kennan became something of a democrat—and an evangelist. He appealed directly to the people and urged them to take action. He suggested not only that the people might know more about this issue than the elites who coolly calculate throw-weights and megatonnage, but also that the people may be in a position to do something about it.

Kennan's position, as contradictory as it may seem, was similar to that of most realists. All of the realists argued that the role of the guardians was to enlighten the people, not speak for them entirely. Further, the realists came to the conclusion that the technical expert did not necessarily make better political or moral decisions than the ordinary citizen. In 1954 Niebuhr wrote, "Considering the vanity of [the] schemes dreamed up by the intellectuals, one is almost persuaded to thank God for the common-sense wisdom of the 'man in the street.'" Niebuhr speculated that a taxi driver might well be superior to many intellectuals "in dealing with the complexities of politics" be-

45. George Kennan, "On Nuclear War" (speech delivered on receipt of the Grenville Clark Prize, November 16, 1981), in Kennan, *Nuclear Delusion*, 192–94.
46. Ronald Steel, "The Statesman of Survival," *Esquire*, CIII (January, 1985), 75.

cause the taxi driver's "shrewd awareness of human foibles" would prevent him from "engaging in [the] vain dreams of self-pity" to which intellectuals often fell victim.[47]

Acheson maintained that leaders did their best work and government performed most smoothly when the people were educated and mobilized. As the people begin to understand the issues being debated, he maintained in 1962, "a very curious, almost inexplicable thing goes on in a democracy[:] the people become more critical." When that happens, the leaders begin to realize that "the people have more sense than [the leaders] thought they had." The final result is that "leaders begin to talk with more sense; the people to understand better; and quickly, very quickly, a consensus begins to form."[48]

The strong leadership for which the realists argued did not discount the role of the individual in the political process. Morgenthau wrote that the responsibility of the political authorities, and especially the president, involved presenting to the people alternative solutions to issues "where scientific knowledge and political judgment meet."[49] The rest was in the hands of the people. The president and his colleagues would take the initiative and bear the immediate responsibility for policy decisions, but the people retained the power to alter the president's policies and bore the long-term responsibility for the nation's actions.

As guardians, all of the realists considered themselves also to be educators. All of them contributed to the public debate through their numerous writings and speeches, and all worked to clarify confusing and complex issues. Their concision and the lucidity of their prose made their ideas readily accessible, as did the wide circulation of their

47. Reinhold Niebuhr, "A Century of Cold War," New Leader, XXXI (August 2, 1954), 13–14.

48. Dean Acheson, "Real and Imagined Handicaps of Our Democracy in the Conduct of Foreign Relations" (speech delivered at the Truman Library, March 31, 1962), in Acheson, This Vast External Realm (New York, 1973), 125–26.

49. Hans Morgenthau, "Decision Making in the Nuclear Age," Bulletin of the Atomic Scientists, XVIII (December, 1962), 8.

writings in newspapers, magazines, journals, and books. Late in his career Lippmann asked himself, "If the country is to be governed by the consent of the governed, then the governed must arrive at opinions about what their governors want them to consent to: How do they do this?"[50] The answer he arrived at was that the governed must have people like himself—journalists—to report and interpret events. Journalists, Lippmann concluded, were educators and as such they were important instruments of democracy.

The realists never resolved the underlying tension that dominated their thinking about democracy and guardianship. Indeed, they based their entire theory on that tension. Democracy and guardianship complemented each other, completing a circle: the people needed guidance from experts; the guardians needed the common-sense criticism, direction, and moral consensus of the people. Neither the people nor the leaders could survive on their own.

In the end, despite the self-serving characteristics of the realists' view of democracy, it can be stated unequivocally that the realists maintained the absolute necessity of democratic review. This fact is often neglected by critics who tend to dwell on the antidemocratic rhetoric that is so immediately recognizable in the realists' work. The realists believed in democracy and participated in it both as political actors and as educators even though it frustrated them. At one time or another, all of the realists criticized various government attempts to hide behind the veil of national security. During the 1960s, for example, Morgenthau, Niebuhr, and Lippmann severely criticized the government for withholding information and lying to the public about various foreign-policy initiatives.[51] While the American government

50. Walter Lippmann, "The Job of the Washington Correspondent," *Atlantic*, CCV (January, 1960), 49.

51. Morgenthau, Niebuhr, and Lippmann were especially vociferous in their denunciations of United States military involvement in Vietnam. See, for example, Lippmann's "Today and Tomorrow" columns throughout the 1960s; Niebuhr's "Reinhold Niebuhr Discusses the War in Vietnam," *New Republic*, CLIV (January 29, 1966), 15–16; and Morgenthau's *A New American Foreign Policy* (New York, 1969), *passim*.

was becoming more secretive, specialized, and compartmentalized than ever, the realists were among the first to criticize it for this insularity.

In arguing for democratic review to be guided by talented leaders like themselves, the realists upheld the validity of a basic American belief: that a nation can be only as good as its people and the values they possess. No amount of leadership, guardianship, or education could make the people something that they were not. The realists were both proud and ashamed of the American people and their values, and this position was reflected in realist views of democracy and guardianship. The realists' criticism of American culture and their fears for its future went back to the fundamental views of human nature and the specialness of America that formed the basis for their philosophy of power. It is fitting to go back to those most basic views in the final chapter of this study.

5 Wise Men as Cultural Critics

> One of the first requirements of clear thinking about our part in world affairs is the recognition that we cannot be more to others than we are to ourselves—that we cannot be a source of hope and inspiration to others against a background of resigned failure and deterioration of life here at home.
>
> —*George Kennan, 1977*

Morgenthau, Niebuhr, Lippmann, Kennan, and Acheson all lived long, prosperous lives, and all became respected elder statesmen. Although their actual political influence may have diminished as the years passed, their stature as "wise men" grew. People looked to them with the respect owed men of wisdom and experience, and the realists responded by continuing to produce important work well into their later years.

As elder statesmen, the realists commanded attention even if they were not always taken seriously by policy makers. At times they wielded significant influence, as when they spoke out against American policy in Vietnam. At other times they were ignored. To many policy makers, the realists must have seemed like bitter old men who did nothing but complain to a public that was too polite or too somnolent to chastise them for their negativism. Their complaints, however, grew out of something deeper than mere frustration over declining influence. These grumblings about American society and foreign policy were central, long-term preoccupations, each of which had its roots in the earliest realist writings.

Calling upon the reservoir of respect they had earned over the years, the aging realists tackled some of the most difficult issues facing modern America. No longer involved in the daily intrigue of political infighting, they could afford to take a broad view of some of the nation's social ills, and armed with a new sense of freedom, most of them found themselves championing causes and positions that challenged mainstream thinking and conventional wisdom. Their stature evolved into something akin to that of prophets: they appeared to have special vision, inspiration, and foresight. Kennan, for one, recognized that people perceived him this way. He went so far as to include Richard Wilbur's poem "Advice to a Prophet" as an epigraph to his 1982 book, *The Nuclear Delusion.*

Besides their impressive works of history, political analysis, and commentary, the realists also produced a literature of cultural criticism worthy of the prophet's mantle. They always had engaged in some cultural criticism amid their other work, but the frequency of such criticism increased as they drifted farther away from the centers of political power. As the amount of criticism increased, so did the severity of its tone. The realists almost always sounded melancholy about the least-attractive aspects of life in America, but as the years went by this plaintive note took on a more desperate quality.

Firm believers in the idea that foreign policy is inextricably linked to domestic affairs, the realists maintained that if the United States had domestic troubles, those troubles were bound to be reflected in its international affairs. As they saw it, the domestic troubles of postwar America threatened the very underpinnings of America's position in the world. If, as Kennan argued in the late 1940s, the challenge facing America in the postwar world was to establish America as "a counterforce of hope, of idealism, and practical determination that can win respect everywhere," then there was much work to be done *within* the nation's borders. In 1949, Kennan concluded that "we are not yet ready to lead the world to salvation." Instead, he suggested, "we have to save ourselves first." [1] This would be the realists' message for the remainder of their years.

1. See for example George Kennan, "American-Soviet Relations" (lecture delivered at the Cleveland meeting of the American Political Science Association, December 29,

"Saving ourselves" meant developing policies for dealing with the domestic problems of unemployment and inflation. Kennan suggested that "there are a whole series of negative phenomena in American life, which, if allowed to continue to become worse, will eventually become intolerable and will call, then, for drastic, expensive solutions."[2] Among the worst aspects of these phenomena, aside from their obvious unattractiveness, was their revelation of internal social weakness. How could America lead, how could it be a beacon of hope, if it were beset with such problems? Kennan confessed in a 1956 speech that he was "not at all comfortable" with the "apparent prosperity" of postwar America. The prosperity, he argued, "embraces—or is accompanied by—too many other things that to my mind are deeply disturbing."[3] Just as the process of democratic governance had its disadvantages when it came to maintaining steady, purposeful foreign policies, so too did the new American prosperity, which brought along with it self-indulgence, poor planning, and numerous social inequities.

The realists determined that it was time to redefine the promise of American life for the modern (nuclear) age. Morgenthau identified the situation as "a crisis of national purpose." In *The Purpose of American Politics* (1960), a book devoted to an exploration of this crisis, Morgenthau wrote, "It is exactly because we are no longer as sure as we used to be of what America stands for, of what distinguishes it from other nations, of what the meaning of its existence is, that we must inquire into its purpose."[4] Such insecurity brought new expressions of America's "purpose" and proposals for seeing that it be fulfilled. Like Kennan, Morgenthau and the other realists concluded that leadership abroad begins at home.

1946), in Box 16, George F. Kennan Papers, Princeton University, Princeton, N.J.; and "Basic Factors in American Foreign Policy" (lecture delivered at Dartmouth College, February 14, 1949), in Box 17, Kennan Papers.

2. George Kennan, *The Cloud of Danger: Current Realities of American Foreign Policy* (Boston, 1977), 19.

3. George Kennan, "Speech to Princeton Stevenson for President Committee" (delivered April 30, 1956), in Box 19, Kennan Papers.

4. Hans Morgenthau, *The Purpose of American Politics* (New York, 1960), 3–4.

Niebuhr was also vocal about forging a redefinition of American goals, and he was especially active in attacking complacency brought on by prosperity. "The more we indulge in an uncritical reverence for the supposed wisdom of the American way of life," he wrote in 1948, "the more odious we make it in the eyes of the world, and the more we destroy our moral authority."[5] Niebuhr's constant diatribes against "the idolatrous devotion" of Americans to their own culture were typical of the realists' efforts as cultural critics.[6] The other realists concurred with Niebuhr both in his complaints and in his commendation of the virtues of constructive self-criticism and reflection.

It may have been Lippmann, however, who made the most dramatic plea for cultural criticism. Appearing in a 1961 interview on CBS television, Lippmann suggested that it might be time for "old men" to start thinking in new directions. Stating that "I don't think old men ought to promote wars for young men to fight," he concluded that "warlike old men" could best serve the country by using "whatever wisdom they [can] find to avert what would be an absolute calamity for the world"— another war.[7] The implication was that old ways of thought no longer would do; leaders had to question their old assumptions as well as the assumptions of the society they were leading. The image of Lippmann, himself an aging warrior, urging others of his generation to be more critical of themselves and their attitudes was a powerful one.

The primary subject of the realists' cultural criticism was their unhappiness with the modern technological age. Suspicious of technology and fearful of its implications, the realists linked it with what they perceived as a decline of the West. They were profoundly dissatisfied with the overwhelming role that technology was playing in shaping the culture and consciousness of Western society. In reaction to the effects of the onslaught of science, they became nostalgic for an earlier time when technology offered more of a hope than a threat.

5. Reinhold Niebuhr, "American Pride and Power," *American Scholar,* XVII (Autumn, 1948), 394.

6. See, for example, Reinhold Niebuhr, "The Idolatry of America," *Christianity and Society,* XV (Spring, 1950), reprinted in Niebuhr, *Love and Justice: Selections from the Shorter Writings of Reinhold Niebuhr* (Philadelphia, 1957), 94–97.

7. Walter Lippmann, *Conversations with Walter Lippmann* (Boston, 1965), 70.

The Decline of the West

The realists' tendency to link technology and the decline of the West manifested itself particularly in their attention to three issues: the sterility of mass culture, the nuclear crisis, and the deterioration of the environment. At the center of their displeasure was the belief that the United States and other Western societies had rushed headlong to the edge of an abyss. They wrote of a maladjusted West that since the Industrial Revolution had been physically and psychologically devastated by technology. Inexorably, in their view, this trend had reached its apotheosis with the development of the atomic bomb and thermonuclear weapons.

At the heart of this critique was an attack on rationalism itself—an attack, in essence, on those who preached the all-powerful redeeming virtues of science and progress. According to the realists, the fruits of science were impressive and worthy of praise, but science itself could not provide the answers to all of man's problems. Western society's worship of science and the "scientific mind" was thus a dangerous development made only more frightening by the presence of all-encompassing technologies such as instruments of mass communication and weapons of mass destruction. There was great urgency in the realists' warnings, most of which pointed to the checkered present that an obsessively rationalist society already had produced.[8]

"When I speak of the nuclear age," wrote Morgenthau, "I am really using a kind of intellectual shorthand, for the availability of nuclear power, particularly for the purposes of war, is but the most spectacular characteristic of an age that has witnessed revolutionary transformations in other fields of technology as well." He pointed out that "technologically speaking," the modern age "really begins with the invention of the steam engine, the railroad, the telegraph, and the machine gun."[9] As Morgenthau portrayed it, scientific progress in itself was neither good nor bad; it had both positive and negative consequences. What was clearly negative about "progress" was the presumption that

8. See, for example, Hans Morgenthau, *Scientific Man Versus Power Politics* (Chicago, 1946).

9. Hans Morgenthau, *Science: Servant or Master?* (New York, 1972), 110.

science somehow supersedes other categories of inquiry—that science is truth and will provide all the answers. The steam engine, railroad, telegraph, and machine gun all represented great strides forward in their particular fields, but they also brought problems along with them—problems that technology by itself could not solve.

What concerned Morgenthau and the other realists most was that technology now seemed to be controlling society rather than society controlling it. The realists feared that Westerners had become slaves to their own inventions, willingly and even hungrily accepting them into their lives without reflecting on the consequences. Technology and progress seemed to be providing some kind of transcendent meaning to those whom they served. The realists turned to poignant examples from their own lives to illustrate their belief that any role society previously might have had as master of its own destiny was now slipping away.

The writings of the realists' later years were filled with references to the magnitude of this problem. In his *Memoirs*, which prefigured *Sketches from a Life*, Kennan emphasized the discontinuities between the past and the present, pinpointing unfettered technological growth as the source of much of his displeasure. In both *Memoirs* and *Sketches*, Kennan alternated between lyrical descriptions of a remembered, idyllic past and forceful accounts of the modern, industrialized landscape. He portrayed an America of striking contrasts: an America where small-town life had been dwarfed and threatened by urbanization and where rural simplicity had given way to faceless technocratic complexity. Kennan presented this evolution as sad and tragically inevitable.[10]

In one respect, there was nothing special about all this. Many people, as they get older, look back wistfully on the past, remembering a simpler time when all seemed right. It is human nature to remember one's youth and think that the snow was deeper, the winter colder, and one's determination stronger. Kennan, so it appeared, suffered from a particularly acute case of this tendency to glorify the past. He often

10. Especially relevant are the two volumes of Kennan's *Memoirs*. See Kennan, *Memoirs, 1925–1950* (Boston, 1967), chaps. 1, 3, 20, and *Memoirs, 1950–1963* (Boston, 1972), chap. 4.

resorted to conjuring up a pastoral arcadia to contrast with the contemporary scene. In doing this he was not merely suffering from a severe case of nostalgia brought on by technological skittishness. He also had an issue to raise with the contemporary world—the issue of control.

Kennan's *Memoirs* and *Sketches* were, in large part, his attempt to find his bearings in a world that was rapidly changing. He revealed his bias early—in the third sentence of the *Memoirs*—when in discussing the difficulties of writing about one's past, he speculated on "whether the immediacy of remembered experience is not impaired by the *ruthless destruction* of setting which explosions of population and technological change have so often worked." [11] Other realists shared Kennan's dilemma and echoed his anxieties. Acheson, for one, sought to recover the lost arcadia of his boyhood in, among other places, his autobiographical sketches in *Morning and Noon* (1965). In these reminiscences, Acheson painted scenes of the idyllic Middletown, Connecticut, of his youth, replete with towering trees, clear streams, and prosperous homes, all unsullied by urban decay and technological complications.

Acheson's nostalgia for the preautomotive age was only occasionally as saccharine as Kennan's, but it was just as detectable throughout his work. At the beginning of *Present at the Creation*, for example, Acheson remarked offhandedly but proudly that he and his colleagues in the old State Department building in the 1940s "stifled under the full blast of the summer sun" without the benefit of "any such newfangled contrivance as air conditioning." [12] There was a not-so-subtle trace of nostalgia in Acheson's voice in that statement and in others like it, as if life were somehow nobler and truer in the days before "newfangled contrivances."

Perhaps the best expression of Kennan's (and the other realists') uneasiness with the modern age was a diary entry, included in his *Memoirs*, that illustrated his sense of alienation. Describing his ire and frustration with passing motorists as he cycled across the Wisconsin

11. Kennan, *Memoirs*, I, 3. Emphasis mine.
12. Dean Acheson, *Present at the Creation: My Years in the State Department* (New York, 1969), 7.

farmland of his boyhood after an extended stay in Europe, Kennan wrote:

> The occupants of the occasional machines that went whirring by . . . obviously had no connection in the social sense with the highway over which they were driving. . . . They were lost spirits, hovering for brief periods on another plane, where space existed only in time. To those of us who inhabited the highway—the birds and insects and snakes and turtles and chipmunks and the lone cyclist—the cars were only an abstract danger, a natural menace like lightning, earthquake, or flood, which had to be reckoned with and coped with (here the turtles, whose corpses strewed the pavement for miles, seemed to be at the greatest disadvantage) but to which we had no human relationship and which only accentuated our . . . loneliness.[13]

Alienation and powerlessness in the face of technological change overwhelmed Kennan. He was more at home with the creatures of the wild and his simple bicycle than with the faceless occupants of those contraptions called automobiles. His loneliness and sense of loss were best expressed in his own words: "It seemed to me that we had impoverished ourselves by the change; and I could not, after the years in Europe, accustom myself to it."[14]

The loss of a pastoral ideal was an underlying theme throughout Kennan's *Memoirs* and *Sketches,* and indeed throughout all of his writings. His use of it was reminiscent of Henry Adams, who in *The Education of Henry Adams* and *Mont St. Michel and Chartres* sought to make sense out of himself and his era by gauging his position in history against a fixed point in the past. For Adams, the "velocity of history," which he measured against the medieval world and the scholastic tradition, was the essential issue. For Kennan, the idealized point of stasis was found in the preindustrial age or, to be more precise, in the age of preindustrial, small-town America—America before highways, gadgetry, or shopping malls. This was also the America of men of character such as Alexander Kirk—a colleague of Kennan's in the Berlin embassy in the early 1940s, later ambassador to Italy and Egypt—

13. Kennan, *Memoirs,* I, 76.
14. *Ibid.*

whom Kennan acknowledged admiringly in the *Memoirs*. Kirk epitomized for Kennan the proper way to live. "The only thing worth living for," Kirk once told Kennan, was "good form."[15] Kennan's ideal world was not only pastoral, but it was also a place where manners and gestures were significant.

The disruption of the pastoral ideal was all to obvious to the realists; they unanimously denounced what Kennan called "the sickly secularism" of modern society and "the appalling shallowness of the religious, philosophic and political concepts that pervade it."[16] Morgenthau decried "the unrestrained and self-sufficient hedonism" that contemporary society promoted. Such hedonism, he believed, was the product of excessive materialism and "production for its own sake." Fashion and style had replaced usefulness as a criterion for the desirability of a product. Wastefulness reigned as old, fixed standards of judgment were abandoned for new, more fashionable ones.[17]

The result was the ruin of the American landscape, the loss of the nation's soul, and the destruction of the social fabric. "This society," said Kennan in a 1976 interview, "bears the seeds of its own horrors—unbreathable air, undrinkable water, starvation—and until people realize we have to get back to a much simpler form of life, a much smaller population, a society in which the agrarian component is far greater again in relation to the urban component—until these appreciations become widespread and effective—I can see no answers to the troubles of our times."[18] Kennan had seen the enemy, and the enemy was us.

"Our people enjoy an abundance of material things, such as no large community of men has ever known," wrote Lippmann in 1954.

15. Kennan, *Memoirs*, II, 114. Although this incident was a minor one and Kirk did not play a significant role in the rest of Kennan's life, the inclusion of Kirk in the *Memoirs* is interesting. This short quotation captures an important aspect of Kennan's outlook on life.

16. George Kennan, *Democracy and the Student Left* (Boston, 1968), 216.

17. Morgenthau, *Purpose of American Politics*, 215.

18. George Kennan, *Encounters with Kennan: The Great Debate*, ed. Daniel Moynihan (London, 1979), 4.

"But our people are not happy about their position or confident about their future. For we are no longer sure whether our responsibilities are not greater than our power and our wisdom."[19] No issue crystallized this anxiety more than the nuclear issue. Here was a responsibility with which, clearly, society was uncomfortable. The nuclear issue became a symbol—or, as Morgenthau put it, "shorthand"—for the many problems that technology and progress brought with them, as well as for the general problem of reconciling power and responsibility in the postwar world.

Will Civilization Survive Technics?

The realists' feared that its love affair with technology was distorting the West's perception of world problems. The unquestioning acceptance of technics invited poor self-discipline, wishful thinking, and an internal "softness" that threatened the West's well-being from within as well as from without. Modern culture, with its lack of historical perspective and its presumption that technology could allay any insecurity, seemed to Niebuhr and the other realists to be "inveterately utopian." Niebuhr complained that "our modern culture is too flat, too lacking in the tragic sense of life, and too blind to the total dimension of existence to be an adequate guide for our day." He argued instead for a culture that accepted the fact that "human life cannot be completely fulfilled in human history"—that nothing, not even the wonders of technology, could change the human condition.[20]

The flatness of modern culture was a result of what Niebuhr called "technocratic illusions." Such illusions came from those who failed to recognize the limitations and the dangers of technics.[21] One of the worst manifestations of this way of thinking was, to the realists' minds,

19. Walter Lippmann, "The Shortage of Education," *Atlantic*, CXCIII (May, 1954), 35–38.
20. Reinhold Niebuhr, "Will Civilization Survive Technics?" *Commentary*, I (December, 1945), 8.
21. Reinhold Niebuhr, "Our Country and Our Culture: A Symposium," *Partisan Review*, XIX (May-June, 1952), 303.

mass culture. The realists found mass culture to be annoyingly reductive and unsatisfactory, largely because it was directed at passive, undifferentiated audiences. Kennan called mass culture "cloying" and described it as "a tremendous, easy, and insidious narcosis, quietly eating away at our capacity for direct experience and at the same time lulling us into a lazy imperviousness to what is really happening to us." He warned that mass culture, and the modern culture of which it was a part, threatened to make us "slaves" rather than "masters of our habits." [22]

In addition to being a barbiturate, mass culture also could be a stimulant—with the worst of side effects. In a May, 1970, speech delivered at the United States Air University at Maxwell Air Force Base in Alabama, Acheson expressed abiding realist anxieties about the role of mass media in American life. Citing the extraordinary pace of change brought about in the news business by the increasing influence of radio and television, Acheson called the new "torrent of information" available to the public overwhelming. He thought that the public lacked a "historical perspective and a prevailing set of values necessary to cope with it." The "new" news media, Acheson believed, were not suited to presenting difficult political issues in all their complexity. The new forms of communication, he argued, encouraged "exhibitionism, extremism, and violence." In obvious reference to the student unrest in full bloom at the time of his speech, he concluded that "the effect [of the electronic media] is to set aflame the atmosphere of political discourse and deprive it of reason, just as the great fire raids of the last war fed upon oxygen sucked from the air."

Acheson ended his speech with a warning: if the people of the United States did not take measures to break through the oversimplifications that passed for political thought and the dramatic gestures that passed for political activity, the future would be grim. "I cannot recall," he stated, "an instance of a democratic society that, once having lost the will to provide for its domestic tranquility and national

22. George Kennan, "Commencement Address: Connecticut College" (delivered June 10, 1956), in Box 19, Kennan Papers.

security, has regained it by a new birth of discipline and commitment." This apparent loss of social control led Acheson to despair. His final words, in the form of a quatrain, were a mixture of a minister's jeremiad, a prophet's warning, and an old man's gloom:

I tell you nought for your comfort
Yea, nought for your desire,
Save that the sky grows darker yet,
And the sea rises higher.[23]

Despite his lapse into melodrama, no one in the audience that day could have doubted the sincerity of Acheson's deep apprehensions about mass culture and its effects on American politics and society.

For Morgenthau, mass communications, mass culture, and mass destruction were all interrelated: all were products of technology, and all led to the alienation of man from his fellow man and from his environment. Mass culture, Morgenthau concluded, was a major contributor to the narcissism so prevalent in the 1970s. Modern society deprived the individual of the "objective rational norms" that in other societies had been abundantly clear. The result was that the individual himself became "the measure of all things" and surrendered to his "raw aspirations." Morgenthau asserted that "without a socially determined role to satisfy," the individual "must increasingly turn to personal satisfaction in its narrow sense." This, Morgenthau believed, was a prescription for cultural (and personal psychological) disaster. The culture was awash in a sea of relativity; people were seeking meaning primarily in themselves. As mass culture droned on in the background, it perpetuated alienation and reinforced the turn to personal satisfaction and narcissism.[24]

Morgenthau's most forceful example of the way in which mass cul-

23. Dean Acheson, "The Changing American Scene" (speech delivered at United States Air University, Maxwell Air Force Base, Alabama, May 13, 1970), in Acheson, *Fragments of My Fleece* (New York, 1971), 185–97.

24. Hans Morgenthau and Ethel Person, "The Roots of Narcissism," *Partisan Review*, XLV (Fall, 1978), 346, 338. This theme is discussed in more detail in Christopher Lasch, *The Culture of Narcissism: American Life in an Age of Diminishing Expectations* (New York, 1979).

ture alienated the individual was his treatment of "death in the nuclear age." He contended that the specter of mass destruction changed man's relationship to nature, to government, and most importantly, to himself. The possibility of nuclear annihilation gave even death a new meaning. Before nuclear weapons, man was to some degree still the master of his own life and death; he could take solace in the fact that his achievements might be remembered and carried on by family and friends after his death; and he could find satisfaction in knowing that while alive he contributed, however humbly, to the ongoing stream of civilization. But a nuclear holocaust would deprive man of this view of life and death. The concepts of individuality and immortality would disappear along with civilization itself. For an individual to die while contributing to society was one thing; for an individual to die as part of the destruction of civilization was another. If civilization did not live on after one's death, that fact deprived life of much of its meaning.[25]

Rather than succumb to utter despair, Morgenthau suggested an approach to these problems that emphasized constructive thought over self-pity. Like his advice on military strategy and arms control, Morgenthau's social analysis accentuated the need for evolutionary social change backed by new modes of thought. He held as his model the German thinker Karl Jaspers, who as Morgenthau characterized him understood the need for man to adapt to "the novel conditions of the technological age." What was needed was "a new man" for the new age, a man who could "create himself step by step, piecemeal, through the absorption of every new experience with which the technological era confronts him." [26] The most important task was learning how to live *with* technology, not at its mercy. This would require not only social growth and change, but also a reassertion of control. Morgenthau titled his 1972 book on this subject *Science: Servant or Master?*. As the question mark in the title indicated, in his mind the issue was still gravely in doubt.

Kennan was the most eloquent and the most adamant of the realists

25. Hans Morgenthau, "Death in the Nuclear Age," *Commentary*, XXXII (September, 1961), 231–34.
26. Morgenthau, *Science: Servant or Master?*, 153.

arguing for the need to reestablish control over technology and its effects. He asked that modern society stop and take a look at itself, then declare itself free from its slavish devotion to new inventions. Nuclear weapons provided him with his best and most appropriate example. The United States government not only had accepted such weapons as a vital component of its armed forces, but it actually had built its defenses around them. Nuclear weapons were spotlighted rather than deemphasized—especially in Europe. By making these weapons such an integral part of its defense strategy, the United States had lost a measure of the control that it might have had over them. As time wore on, a pledge of "no first use" became increasingly difficult to make, as did any other gesture toward control. In fact, in accepting nuclear weapons as a remedy for conventional imbalances in Europe rather than approaching them as part of the overall political-military problem, the United States had created a whole new set of problems.

Kennan hoped that the United States would have the courage *not* to rely on a first-use strategy and instead to take bold steps to stop the momentum of the arms race. These things, according to Kennan, could be achieved only when the United States strengthened its resolve to achieve them. The issue was one of moral fiber: in Kennan's view, moral fiber was America's first and last line of defense. Technology often chipped away at that fiber and tested the nation's resolve, but it did not always have to win. Kennan suggested that what was needed was a stricter review of technology, a more careful analysis of its effects. He thought that when Americans became aware of what the miracles of technology were actually doing to them, they might not be so enamored with them and would stop seeing them as an "answer."

Kennan did not believe that the clock could be turned back or that technological achievements could be undone, although at times it appeared that he wished that they could. He did believe, however, that some good could be done in this vein. One of his more noteworthy suggestions was presented in 1970 in a *Foreign Affairs* article, "To Prevent a World Wasteland." Here Kennan outlined a proposal for an international environmental agency to oversee new initiatives to clean up pollution on a world-wide scale. As he conceived it, this agency was to be a self-initiated, self-contained, and self-controlled entity, capable of decisive action. Proceeding from "a relatively small group of governments," primarily those of the industrial powers, it would avoid, Kennan hoped, the problems and constraints that had hampered the efforts of similar agencies sponsored by the United Nations. At the end of the proposal, Kennan stated that the Western and Communist powers had an obligation to join forces on this problem. Both East and West, he wrote, needed "to replace the waning fixations of the cold war with interests which they can pursue in common and to everyone's benefit." The problem of global pollution superseded the problem of containment; it was a problem that no one could afford to ignore.[27]

Another somewhat provocative example of how Kennan envisioned modern society overcoming the all-encompassing nature of technology was his suggestion for higher education. Put forth rather casually in *Democracy and the Student Left* and again in his 1976 interview with George Urban, this was not a proposal in a formal sense, but it did reveal Kennan's sympathies. Its essence was that there ought to be some colleges, based on the idea of the old Graduate College at Princeton, where "different" rules prevail. Kennan described such an institution as "an austere place of study":

> We will have no prearranged sporting activities. You can go out and take a walk or play tennis, but no football, no baseball, no mass audiences. This is going to be a place of contemplation. Our terms will be short, as in England, but while you are here, no one, either faculty or students, will leave this place for weekends. You are going to remain here, and we will not have music played all over the campus, nor are we going to have high fidelity equipment installed in your rooms. We will exclude television and all other trivia of mass communication.[28]

Although this monastic endeavor sounded bleak, Kennan did emphasize its voluntary aspect and limited duration.

This proposal for higher education presented Kennan at both his

27. George Kennan, "To Prevent a World Wasteland," *Foreign Affairs*, XLVIII (April, 1970), 410, 413.
28. Kennan, *Encounters with Kennan*, 49.

165

best and his worst. He was at his best in showing one way to assert mastery over technology. (Granted it was temporary mastery and mastery through abstention, but it was mastery nevertheless.) Kennan was at his worst in suggesting that technology is an enemy—that television and high-fidelity equipment must be avoided if one is to find truth and virtue. Coexistence was not mentioned, nor was the possibility that some good could come out of contact with technology. Redemption was to be found in the pastoral, the agrarian, and the nontechnological—and for Kennan, the way to find it was through pietistic denial.

When Kennan indulged himself in a single-minded denunciation of anything technological, his critique ceased to be useful. It is disappointing that neither he nor any of the other realists gave more credit to technology for the positive things it had produced: better health care and the means to verify arms-control agreements, to name just two examples. This shortcoming, however, did little to diminish the force of Kennan's message: the West, and particularly the United States, had to stop worshiping the gods of technology and unlimited economic growth. Kennan saw complete folly in the notion that America's problems could be solved by growing out of them or by depending on the next invention to be a savior.[29] The nation's and the world's problems could be solved only by the people behind the inventions, people who had to use the fruits of their knowledge wisely.

Morgenthau was a bit more generous toward technology; he was willing to consider its potential with more optimism than Kennan. He agreed with Kennan that technology and the "scientific mind" were the roots of much evil, but he was willing to be more flexible in accepting both phenomena as realities of modern life. Morgenthau was able to bring himself to look to the future, whereas Kennan was bent on looking back to the past. Morgenthau considered technology to have a "Janus head." On one side, "it has enormously broadened and disseminated man's understanding of himself and his environment," he wrote, "while on the other it has unleashed destructive forces which man has thus far proven unable to harness for human needs."[30] As he saw it,

29. See Kennan interview with Melvin J. Lasky, *ibid.*, 189–215.
30. Morgenthau and Person, "Roots of Narcissism," 340.

technology offered possibilities as well as problems, and it was his duty to explore both.

Morgenthau refused to be sentimental or nostalgic about the past; he did not share Kennan's view that the preindustrial age was a golden one. References to a golden age were, he thought, the work of political romantics of all stripes, but certainly not of realists. A tendency to exalt the past was dangerous. Not only was it wishful thinking, but it usually led to a distortion of the past that was of little use in solving contemporary problems. The road to the future was not through the past. Modern society could learn from the past, but it had to proceed directly to the future without taking psychological detours to a golden age that probably never existed anyway.

Morgenthau frequently lambasted political romantics, especially politically conservative ones. Kennan escaped direct criticism for his romanticism, but figures such as Barry Goldwater, the senator and presidential candidate, did not. In Morgenthau's opinion, Goldwater was the consummate political romantic. "The political romantic," Morgenthau wrote in reference to Goldwater in 1964, "carries within himself the picture of a glorious past, fancied or real or both, of a golden age once possessed and now lost." The problem with this, argued Morgenthau, was that it involved a static world view with no allowance for growth. "This picture," he continued, "provides the romantic with the standards for political judgment, the goals for political action, the arguments and imagery of political rhetoric. The past was great and simple; the present is complexity, decline, and decadence; the future will be great and simple again by being like the past."[31] Morgenthau resisted such reasoning and exposed its fallacies at every turn. Perhaps because his own past was far from idyllic, he had great difficulty swallowing the political romantic's reverence for bygone days. Morgenthau identified the political romantic's worship of the past as equivalent to the scientific man's worship of science, technology, and the future: both outlooks were simplistic and utopian.

31. Hans Morgenthau, "Goldwater: The Romantic Regression," *Commentary*, XXXVIII (September, 1964), 65.

Civilization would survive technics only if it could maintain control over new technologies. For Acheson and Kennan, such control depended upon keeping up a healthy skepticism of technology and refusing to accept some of its more egregious manifestations. Both men invoked the past to illustrate how much damage already had been done, but for Morgenthau, control had less to do with the past than with the present and future. He was concerned with making the most of technology's possibilities while minimizing its risks. Any reference to a golden age of the past or a utopia of the future based on scientific progress was, to him, an anathema. Morgenthau (and Kennan, despite his reveries) understood that the key to the future—and the key to controlling technology—lay within Western culture itself. Attitudes had to change, the social implications of new technologies had to be explored, and restraint had to be considered. Reassessments had to be made, and the best place to begin was at home.

America as Example: City on a Hill

Like generations of Americans before them, the realists wanted to make America an example that the rest of the world would wish to follow. Prestige, they believed, did not depend solely on military might. Prestige depended on the image that America presented to the world—the success of the American experiment, the American idea. As Lippmann said in a 1965 television interview, the days when the United States could be the world's "policeman" were over. "We are not able to run the world, and we shouldn't pretend that we can," he declared. "Let us tend to our own business, which is great enough." Declaring that "our education is inadequate, our cities badly built, [and] our social arrangements unsatisfactory," Lippmann suggested that it was time for the United States to take seriously the idea that foreign policy begins on the domestic scene.[32]

As Lippmann saw it, domestic tranquility, prosperity, and social justice had to prevail within the United States before Americans could

32. Lippmann, *Conversations*, 231–32.

hope to effect change in Asia, Europe, and the third world. At about this same time, Morgenthau identified eight major domestic issues he considered to be critical: nuclear energy, economics, race relations, health care, education, the deterioration of cities, the environment, and the future of democratic government. Morgenthau spent much of his later years reflecting on the importance of these problems, often pleading for attention to points that he considered painfully obvious but that others seemed to be willfully overlooking. His involvement with the Americans for Democratic Action and his editing of the ADA-sponsored *Crossroad Papers* (1965), which dealt with these issues, grew out of his discontent with the status quo. Believing that the United States could and should do better in its domestic affairs, he took part in shaping specific proposals toward that end.

Morgenthau's criticism was severe enough, but it did not approach the indignation registered by Kennan. Like the other realists, Kennan subscribed to the belief that "in world affairs, as in personal life, example exerts a greater power than precept." It was unfortunate, he thought, that the United States was providing such a poor example. The older he got, the worse the situation seemed to be, and by the 1980s, it seemed to have become intolerable.

In the mid-1980s, in a widely noted *Foreign Affairs* article, "Morality and Foreign Policy," Kennan singled out fiscal irresponsibility as the latest instance of social weakness in America:

A country that has a budgetary deficit and an adverse trade balance both so fantastically high that it is rapidly changing from a major creditor to a major debtor on the world's exchanges, a country whose own enormous internal indebtedness has been permitted to double in less than six years, a country that has permitted its military expenditures to grow so badly out of relationship to other needs of its economy and so extensively out of reach of political control that the annual spending of hundreds of billions of dollars on "defense" has developed into a national addiction—a country that, in short, has allowed its financial and material affairs to drift into such disorder, is so obviously living beyond its means, and confesses itself unable to live otherwise—is simply not in a position to make the most effective use of its own resources on the international scene, because they are so largely out of its control.[33]

This loss of national self-control was staggering, but not out of character. In Kennan's opinion, it was the latest in a series of irresponsible acts, noteworthy more for the immensity of its proportions than its slothfulness.

Kennan and the other realists thought it was their duty to point out slothfulness when they saw it and to work for its abolition whenever possible. They took it upon themselves to make sure that America lived up to its professed ideals, that it backed its rhetoric with action. As American exceptionalists they believed in an America that had high moral values and standards—standards by which all of its actions had to be judged. Their jeremiads on the unhealthy state of American culture served a dual purpose: to warn and to affirm. The realists warned that if the United States lost its soul, it would not be able to exercise its power responsibly. In the process, they also affirmed the righteousness of the ideals embodied in their notion of responsible power.

In a 1952 letter to Arnold Toynbee, Kennan succinctly summarized his view on morality and American exceptionalism. "I think we know what, for us, is right and wrong," he wrote. "I believe that 'right' consists in our being faithful to our best and simplest and most genuine American traditions, which most of us understand quite well." On the other hand, he continued, "I do not think we can expect to know what is right or wrong in the behavior of other peoples."[34] Kennan believed that Americans should reserve their moral judgments primarily for themselves. He thought it was foolish for Americans to hold other nations to an American code of behavior, especially when America itself so often failed to meet its own standards.

In 1969, Morgenthau echoed these sentiments in a short piece titled "The Present Tragedy of America," written for *Worldview* mag-

33. George Kennan, "Morality and Foreign Policy," *Foreign Affairs*, LXIV (Winter, 1985–86), 215–16.
34. George Kennan to Arnold Toynbee, March 18, 1952, in Box 29, Kennan Papers.

azine. The "tragedy" he referred to was the so-called moral crisis in America, a crisis brought on by the incongruity between America's moral standards and its behavior. Morgenthau wrote that "the way a country lives up to its pretenses, or the way it does not live up to its pretenses, has a direct relevance upon its position amongst nations." In other words, "the United States, in a unique sense, is being judged by other nations, and it is being judged by itself in terms of its compliance with the moral standards it has set for itself." The immediate failure in 1969 was American policy in Vietnam; Morgenthau considered this policy to be a "betrayal" of American ideals. America could not be the "last best hope of mankind" when it pursued such policies and set such a dubious example.[35] Other failures were to follow, particularly in the area of nuclear weapons.

As Kennan wrote in 1986, the best place to "seek possibilities for service to morality" was "primarily in our own behavior, not in our judgment of others."[36] All the realists shared this view; morality for them was something that came from within and could not be imposed from the outside. Connected to this was their recognition of the importance of limits. The realists often quoted John Quincy Adams' warning that although the United States could be the friend of liberty throughout the world, it could not be the "guarantor" of liberty for all peoples.[37] They understood that the United States, no matter how powerful it was, could not bear the world's burdens. The realists spent their later years reiterating their contention that, paradoxically, the United States had to put limits on itself (and its technology) if it were to be a forceful world leader.

Forty years after his "X" article made *containment* a household word, Kennan attempted to modify the idea and adapt it to a new set of problems. When *Foreign Affairs* reprinted "The Sources of Soviet Conduct" in 1987 as part of a group of articles commemorating the fortieth anniversary of its original publication, the issue also included

35. Hans Morgenthau, "The Present Tragedy of America," *Worldview*, XII (September, 1969), 14.
36. Kennan, "Morality and Foreign Policy," 217.
37. See, for example, Kennan's use of Adams in *Cloud of Danger*, 43.

a new piece by Kennan outlining his latest thoughts on the meaning of containment. In this updated evaluation, Kennan wrote that "what needs most to be contained, as I see it, is not so much the Soviet Union but the weapons race itself." He cited several other candidates for containment: "fanatical and wildly destructive religious fundamentalism," terrorism, the "rapid depletion of the world's nonrenewable energy resources," the "steady pollution of [the world's] atmosphere and its waters," and the "general deterioration of [the] environment as a support system for civilized living."[38] Kennan believed that most of these problems, especially those concerning weapons, technology, and the environment, could be contained—or at least could begin to be contained—through self-restraint and purposeful unilateral action.

In 1986 Kennan asked rhetorically whether there is "any such thing as morality that does not rest, consciously or otherwise, on some foundation of religious faith, for the renunciation of self-interest, which is what all morality implies, can never be rationalized by purely secular and materialistic considerations."[39] The realists were all, in their own ways, men of faith. They did not ask the United States to renounce its self-interest, but neither did they recommend that the nation stockpile all the weapons it could, brandish its arsenal boldly, or use its power in a confrontational manner. Power, especially the raw scientific and military power embodied in nuclear weaponry, meant little when separated from considerations of morality and responsibility.

Although this study has concentrated on power in its most literal manifestation, the realist idea of responsible power was not limited to the nuclear realm. The idea surfaced in other areas as well, most notably in the use of conventional military force and in regard to political and economic influence. An analysis of the realists' views on the use of force in interventions such as those in Korea, Latin America, and most significantly, Vietnam, would yield a version of responsible power quite similar to the one they applied to nuclear weapons. So would discussions of the realists' positions on the uses of political and economic

38. George Kennan, "Containment Then and Now," *Foreign Affairs*, LXIV (Winter, 1985–86), 889.

39. Kennan, "Morality and Foreign Policy," 217.

power as exercised in the Marshall Plan, in numerous foreign-aid programs, and in the imposition of economic sanctions.

Usable and unusable force, the nuclear dilemma, and the impact of science and technology were merely the most visible examples of the realists' preoccupation with moral values; they were the issues that put into sharpest relief the moral concerns implicit in all of the realists' versions of the national interest, as well as in their views on other specific policy matters. Much more could be written—for example, on how power and responsibility were reconciled in the realists' treatment of human-rights issues, on the status of international law, and on realist views concerning the propriety of intervention. It was no accident that the realists devoted so much attention to these issues, all of which by definition have a heavy normative or ethical component. Nor was it any accident that in every case, the realists reached conclusions that were as dependent on moral reasoning as on pure geopolitical or practical calculations. If there was one constant running through all of their work, it was that the "moral" and the "practical" could not be separated. As a result, the realists seemed attracted to those most difficult issues where morality and pragmatism were tortuously intertwined. Asking Americans for self-restraint and reasoned reflection on their own values was the ultimate expression of the quest for responsible power: it called for a mature America that could see beyond its immediate self-interest and conquer its urge for instant gratification.

The Realist Legacy

Except for George Kennan, the realists included in this study have passed from the scene. Acheson and Niebuhr died in 1971, both at the age of 78; Lippmann in 1974 at the age of 85; and Morgenthau in 1980 at the age of 76. Although Kennan continues to carry on the realist tradition in impressive style, he is very much alone. Self-proclaimed neorealists have pursued lines of their own, but none of them possesses the world view and life experiences of the original postwar realists, and their enterprise has developed into something quite different from that first outlined by Morgenthau in 1948.[40] Born in the late nineteenth and early twentieth centuries, the original postwar American realists matured in a world very different from that of the past half-century, and their political thought reflected their cultural biases.

The revelation of these biases in no way negates the achievements of the realists. In fact, it makes their achievements (and shortcomings) that much plainer. With an understanding of the realists' backgrounds and a synthesis of their points of view in hand, it becomes possible to see postwar American realism in its full context, as a product of the milieu in which it was formed. Obvious anachronisms notwithstanding, the realists' ideas about power and responsibility in the nuclear age have resonance and are worthy of careful consideration even today.[41]

In finding the locus of responsibility in the "public philosophy," the realists began with the premise that a relatively stable consensus does exist within the American polity, and that this consensus is sufficiently coherent to serve as a guide to citizen and statesman alike. The consensus no doubt evolves as conditions change, but certain core elements remain. For the postwar realists, the values embodied in the public philosophy were constructed out of the virtues of prudence, humility, the good-faith effort to balance ideals and self-interests, and the preservation of freedom as expressed in the idea of democracy. This last point led inevitably to the promotion of values such as those listed in the nation's founding documents (*e.g.*, the Declaration of Independence and the Bill of Rights), as well as of more general values such as philosophical reflection on ends and means and the idea that the individual must see himself as but one link in the stream of civilization—

40. For an overview of the neorealist school, see Robert Keohane, *Neorealism and Its Critics* (New York, 1986).

41. The realists recognized the potential danger of incorporating one's own personal hierarchy of values into ideas of the national interest. Their insistence on humility, and their diatribes against crusading moralism, were vital counterweights to this dangerous tendency. Also, their belief that private and public morality were linked and yet were not one and the same enabled them to escape the temptation to equate the two or, even worse, to declare them separate spheres.

a product of history with obligations to the past, present, and future. The realists' world view and all of the policy recommendations that arose from it can be traced back to these concerns. The realists' careful attention to the integrity of American domestic structures and concomitant values was not without purpose; it was these structures and values that gave form to the realists' work.

Filtering their decisions through this framework, the realists insisted that the national interest could and should be an expression of American values. "Realism" and "the national interest" were self-consciously loaded terms, both implying a hierarchy of values and subjective judgments. Perhaps the greatest flaw in the realists' own work was their inability to be sufficiently clear in making these values explicit and in acknowledging that such values formed the basis of their version of realpolitik. But rather than lament the subjective nature of realism, it may be more useful to look at this subjectivity—this insistence on the fundamental importance of values—as the heart of the realist enterprise. Here is where the paradoxes and great quandaries of moral leadership have been played out, and this fact helps to explain how individual policy differences (and even differences within the career of one man, as in the case of Kennan) can emerge from the same philosophical commitment.

Despite Morgenthau's audacious and tantalizing attempts, the realists never did succeed in molding decision making and politics among nations into objective sciences: they never succeeded in constructing a set of principles that could bypass or surmount the paradoxes of political morality. Instead, the realists held on to those paradoxes, making them the strength, rather than the weakness, of their thinking. Both in their descriptions of how politics among nations is conducted and in their prescriptions for how it ought to be pursued, what the realists did achieve was the establishment of a model that made possible a reasoned integration of values questions with decision making in international affairs. In embracing rather than rejecting paradox, the realists understood that ethics in international affairs is about evaluating competing moral claims and standing for those values determined to be primary. Their elevation of Weber's "ethic of responsibility," accompanied by their ideas on what such responsibility—or accountability—entailed, made realism in postwar America an instrument not for the avoidance of moral leadership, but for its ultimate fulfillment.

Selected Bibliography

I. DEAN ACHESON

MANUSCRIPTS
Acheson, Dean. Papers. Yale University, New Haven.

BOOKS BY ACHESON
A Citizen Looks at Congress. New York, 1957.
A Democrat Looks at His Party. New York, 1955.
Fragments of My Fleece. New York, 1971.
Grapes from Thorns. New York, 1972.
Morning and Noon. Boston, 1965.
The Pattern of Responsibility. Edited by McGeorge Bundy. Boston, 1952.
Power and Diplomacy. Cambridge, Mass., 1958.
Present at the Creation: My Years in the State Department. New York, 1969.
Sketches from Life of Men I Have Known. New York, 1961.
This Vast External Realm. New York, 1973.

SELECTED ARTICLES BY ACHESON
"A Citizen Takes a Hard Look at the ABM Debate." Washington *Star,* July 27, 1969. Box 54, Dean Acheson Papers. Yale University, New Haven.
"NATO and Nuclear Weapons." *New Republic,* CXXXVII (December 30, 1957), 14–16.

CRITICAL WORKS ON ACHESON
McClellan, David. *Dean Acheson: The State Department Years.* New York, 1976.
Smith, Gaddis. *Dean Acheson.* New York, 1972.
Steel, Ronald. "Acheson at the Creation." *Esquire,* C (December, 1983), 206–15.

II. GEORGE KENNAN

MANUSCRIPTS
Kennan, George F. Papers. Princeton University, Princeton, N.J.

BOOKS BY KENNAN
American Diplomacy. Rev. ed. Chicago, 1984.
The Cloud of Danger: Current Realities of American Foreign Policy. Boston, 1977.
Democracy and the Student Left. Boston, 1968.
Encounters with Kennan: The Great Debate. Edited by Daniel Moynihan. London, 1979.
Memoirs, 1925–1950 (Volume I). Boston, 1967.
Memoirs, 1950–1963 (Volume II). Boston, 1972.
The Nuclear Delusion: Soviet-American Relations in the Atomic Age. New York, 1982.
On Dealing with the Communist World. New York, 1964.
Realities of American Foreign Policy. Princeton, 1954.
Russia, the Atom, and the West. New York, 1957.
Russia and the West Under Lenin and Stalin. Boston, 1960.
Sketches from a Life. New York, 1989.

SELECTED ARTICLES BY KENNAN
"Back from the Brink." With McGeorge Bundy, Robert McNamara, and Gerard Smith. *Atlantic,* CCLVIII (August, 1986), 35–41.
"Containment Then and Now." *Foreign Affairs,* LXV (Spring, 1987), 885–90.
"History as Literature." *Encounter,* XII (April, 1959), 10–16.
"Morality and Foreign Policy." *Foreign Affairs,* LXIV (Winter, 1985–86), 205–19.
"Nuclear Weapons and the Atlantic Alliance." With McGeorge Bundy, Robert McNamara, and Gerard Smith. *Foreign Affairs,* LX (Spring, 1982), 753–68.
"Rebels Without a Program." *New York Times Magazine,* January 21, 1968, p. 22–23, 60–61, 69–71.
"To Ban the H-Bomb Tests." *New York Times,* October 28, 1956, Sec. 4, p. 10.
"To Prevent a World Wasteland." *Foreign Affairs,* XLVIII (April, 1970), 401–13.

CRITICAL WORKS ON KENNAN
Gellman, Barton. *Contending with Kennan: Toward a Philosophy of American Power.* New York, 1984.

Herken, Gregg. "The Great Foreign Policy Fight." *American Heritage,* XXXVII (April–May, 1986), 65–80.

Mayers, David. *George Kennan and the Dilemmas of U.S. Foreign Policy.* New York, 1989.

Steel, Ronald. "The Statesman of Survival." *Esquire,* CIII (January, 1985), 68–75.

Stephanson, Anders. *Kennan and the Art of Foreign Policy.* Cambridge, Mass., 1989.

III. WALTER LIPPMANN

MANUSCRIPTS
Lippmann, Walter. Papers. Yale University, New Haven.

BOOKS BY LIPPMANN
The Cold War: A Study in U.S. Foreign Policy. Boston, 1947.

The Coming Tests with Russia. Boston, 1961.

The Communist World and Ours. Boston, 1959.

Conversations with Walter Lippmann. Boston, 1965.

Drift and Mastery: An Attempt to Diagnose the Current Unrest. New York, 1914.

Essays in the Public Philosophy. Boston, 1955.

The Essential Lippmann: A Political Philosopher for Liberal Democracy. Edited by Clinton Rossiter and James Lare. Cambridge, Mass., 1982.

The Good Society. Boston, 1937.

Interpretations, 1931–1932. Compiled and edited by Allan Nevins. New York, 1933.

Interpretations, 1932–1935. Compiled and edited by Allan Nevins. New York, 1936.

Isolation and Alliances: An American Speaks to the British. Boston, 1952.

The Phantom Public: A Sequel to "Public Opinion." New York, 1927.

A Preface to Morals. New York, 1929.

A Preface to Politics. New York, 1913.

Public Opinion. New York, 1922.

The Stakes of Diplomacy. New York, 1915.

U.S. Foreign Policy: Shield of the Republic. Boston, 1943.

U.S. War Aims. Boston, 1944.

CRITICAL WORKS ON LIPPMANN
Blum, D. Steven. *Walter Lippmann: Cosmopolitanism in the Century of Total War.* Ithaca, 1984.

Childs, Marquis, ed. *Walter Lippmann and His Times.* New York, 1959.
Steel, Ronald. *Walter Lippmann and the American Century.* Boston, 1980.
Wellborn, Charles. *Twentieth Century Pilgrimage: Walter Lippmann and the Public Philosophy.* Baton Rouge, 1969.
Wright, Benjamin. *Five Public Philosophies of Walter Lippmann.* Austin, 1973.

IV. HANS MORGENTHAU

MANUSCRIPTS
Morgenthau, Hans. Papers. Library of Congress, Washington, D.C., and University of Virginia, Charlottesville.

BOOKS BY MORGENTHAU
The Crossroad Papers: A Look into the American Future. New York, 1965.
Dilemmas of Politics. Chicago, 1958.
Essays on Lincoln's Faith and Politics. Lanham, Md., 1983.
In Defense of the National Interest: A Critical Examination of American Foreign Policy. New York, 1951.
A New Foreign Policy for the United States. New York, 1969.
Politics Among Nations: The Struggle for Power and Peace. 1st, 2d, 6th editions. New York, 1948, 1954, 1985.
Principles and Problems in International Politics: Selected Readings. New York, 1950.
The Purpose of American Politics. New York, 1960.
Science: Servant or Master? New York, 1972.
Scientific Man Versus Power Politics. Chicago, 1946.
Truth and Power: Essays of a Decade. New York, 1970.

SELECTED ARTICLES BY MORGENTHAU
"Atomic Force and American Foreign Policy." *Commentary,* XXIII (June, 1957), 501–505.
"The Conduct of American Foreign Policy." *Parliamentary Affairs,* III (Winter, 1949), 147–61.
"Congress and Foreign Policy." *New Republic,* CLX (June, 1960), 16–18.
"Decision Making in the Nuclear Age." *Bulletin of the Atomic Scientists,* XVIII (December, 1962), 7–8.
"The Decline of Democratic Government." *New Republic,* CLXXI (November 9, 1974), 13–18.

"The Dilemma of SALT." *Newsletter: National Commission on American Foreign Policy*, II (August, 1979). Box 109, Hans Morgenthau Papers. University of Virginia, Charlottesville.

"The Evil of Politics and the Ethics of Evil." *Ethics*, LVI (October, 1945), 1–18.

"Goldwater: The Romantic Regression." *Commentary*, XXXVIII (September, 1964), 65–68.

"The H-Bomb and After." *Bulletin of the Atomic Scientists*, VI (March, 1950), 76–79.

"Peace in Our Time?" *Commentary*, XXXVII (March, 1964), 66–69.

"The Political and Military Strategy of the U.S." *Bulletin of the Atomic Scientists*, X (October, 1954), 323–27.

"Power Politics." *Nation*, CLXX (May 20, 1950), 486–87.

"The Present Tragedy of America." *Worldview*, XII (September, 1969), 14–15.

"The Roots of Narcissism." With Ethel Person. *Partisan Review*, XLV (Fall, 1978), 337–47.

CRITICAL WORKS ON MORGENTHAU

Hoffmann, Stanley. "An American Social Science: International Relations." *Daedalus*, CVI (Summer, 1977), 41–60.

————. "Notes on the Limits of Realism." *Social Research*, XLVIII (Winter, 1981), 653–59.

Mastny, Vojtech. *Power and Policy in Transition: Essays Presented on the Tenth Anniversary of the National Committee on American Foreign Policy in Honor of Its Founder, Hans J. Morgenthau*. Westport, Conn., 1984.

Thompson, Kenneth W., and Robert J. Myers, eds. *Truth and Tragedy: A Tribute to Hans Morgenthau*. New Brunswick, N.J., 1984.

V. REINHOLD NIEBUHR

BOOKS BY NIEBUHR

The Children of Light and the Children of Darkness: A Vindication of Democracy and a Critique of Its Traditional Defense. New York, 1944.

Christian Realism and Political Problems. New York, 1953.

Christianity and Power Politics. New York, 1940.

The Essential Reinhold Niebuhr: Selected Essays and Addresses. Edited by Robert McAfee Brown. New Haven, 1986.

Faith and History: A Comparison of Christian and Modern Views of History. New York, 1949.

Selected Bibliography

The Godly and the UnGodly: Essays on the Religious and Secular Dimensions of Modern Life. London, 1959.

An Interpretation of Christian Ethics. New York, 1935.

The Irony of American History. New York, 1952.

Leaves from the Notebook of a Tamed Cynic. Chicago, 1929.

Love and Justice: Selections from the Shorter Writings of Reinhold Niebuhr. Philadelphia, 1957.

Moral Man and Immoral Society: A Study in Ethics and Politics. New York, 1932.

A Nation So Conceived: Reflections on the History of America from Its Early Visions to Its Present Power. With Alan Heimert. New York, 1963.

The Nature and Destiny of Man: A Christian Interpretation. 2 vols. New York, 1941, 1943.

Pious and Secular America. New York, 1958.

Reflections on the End of an Era. New York, 1934.

The Structure of Nations and Empires: A Study of the Recurring Patterns and Problems of the Political Order in Relation to the Unique Problems of the Nuclear Age. New York, 1959.

SELECTED ARTICLES BY NIEBUHR

"American Pride and Power." *American Scholar,* XVII (Autumn, 1948), 393–94.

"A Century of Cold War." *New Leader,* XXXI (August 2, 1954), 12–14.

"The Ethics of War and Peace in the Nuclear Age." With Hans Morgenthau. *War/Peace Report,* VII (February, 1967), 3–8.

"One World or None." *Christianity and Crisis,* VIII (February 16, 1948), 9–10.

"Our Country and Our Culture: A Symposium." *Partisan Review,* XIX (May–June, 1952), 282–326.

"Perils of American Power." *Atlantic,* CXLIX (January, 1932), 90–96.

"Some Things I Have Learned." *Saturday Review,* XLVIII (November 6, 1965), 21–22.

"Test Ban Agreement." *Christianity and Crisis,* XXIII (September 16, 1963), 155.

"Will Civilization Survive Technics?" *Commentary,* I (December, 1945), 2–8.

CRITICAL WORKS ON NIEBUHR

Bingham, June. *Courage to Change: An Introduction to the Life and Thought of Reinhold Niebuhr.* New York, 1972.

Davis, Harry Rex. *The Political Philosophy of Reinhold Niebuhr.* Chicago, 1951.

Fox, Richard. *Reinhold Niebuhr: A Biography.* New York, 1985.

182

Kegley, Charles, and Robert Bretall, eds. *Reinhold Niebuhr: His Religious, Social, and Political Thought.* New York, 1958.

Landon, Harold, ed. *Reinhold Niebuhr: A Prophetic Voice in Our Time.* Greenwich, Conn., 1962.

VI. RELATED WORKS

GENERAL

Clausewitz, Karl von. *On War.* 1832. Rpr. Princeton, N.J., 1976.

Halle, Louis. *The Nature of Power: Civilization and Foreign Policy.* New York, 1955.

Isaacson, Walter, and Evan Thomas. *The Wise Men: Six Friends and the World They Made: Acheson, Bohlen, Harriman, Kennan, Lovett, McCloy.* New York, 1986.

Kissinger, Henry. *American Foreign Policy.* New York, 1974.

———. *Nuclear Weapons and Foreign Policy.* New York, 1957.

———. *A World Restored.* Boston, 1957.

Lilienthal, David. *The Journals of David E. Lilienthal: The Atomic Energy Years, 1945–1950.* Vol. II of 7 vols. New York, 1964.

Masters, Dexter, ed. *One World or None.* New York, 1946.

Oppenheimer, J. Robert. *The Open Mind.* New York, 1955.

Pells, Richard H. *The Liberal Mind in a Conservative Age: American Intellectuals in the 1940s and 1950s.* New York, 1985.

Schlesinger, Arthur M., Jr. *The Vital Center: The Politics of Freedom.* Boston, 1949. Rev. ed., 1962.

Smith, Michael J. *Realist Thought from Weber to Kissinger.* Baton Rouge, 1986.

Thompson, Kenneth W. *Political Realism and the Crisis of World Politics: An American Approach to World Politics.* Princeton, 1960.

U.S. Strategic Bombing Survey. *Overall Report: European War.* Washington, D.C., 1945.

U.S. Strategic Bombing Survey. *Summary Report: Pacific War.* Washington, D.C., 1946.

Weber, Max. *From Max Weber: Essays in Sociology.* Edited by H. H. Gerth and C. Wright Mills. New York, 1958.

CRITICAL WORKS ON NUCLEAR WEAPONS AND AMERICAN FOREIGN POLICY

Alperovitz, Gar. *Atomic Diplomacy: Hiroshima and Potsdam: The Use of the Atomic Bomb and the American Confrontation with Soviet Power.* New York, 1965.

Selected Bibliography

Arneson, R. Gordon. "The H-Bomb Decision." *Foreign Service Journal*, XLVI (May, 1969), 27–29; (June, 1969), 24–27, 43.

Bernstein, Barton, ed. *The Atomic Bomb*. Boston, 1976.

Boyer, Paul. *By the Bomb's Early Light: American Thought and Culture at the Dawn of the Atomic Age*. New York, 1985.

Brodie, Bernard. *War and Politics*. New York, 1973.

Dahl, Robert. *Controlling Nuclear Weapons: Democracy Versus Guardianship*. Syracuse, N.Y., 1985.

Divine, Robert. *Blowing on the Wind: The Nuclear Test Ban Debate, 1945–1960*. New York, 1978.

Dulles, John Foster. "A Policy of Boldness." *Life*, XXXII (May 19, 1952), 146–60.

Fallows, James. *National Defense*. New York, 1981.

Feld, Werner. *Congress and the National Defense: The Politics of the Unthinkable*. New York, 1985.

Freedman, Lawrence. *The Evolution of Nuclear Strategy*. New York, 1982.

Gaddis, John L. *Strategies of Containment: A Critical Appraisal of Postwar American National Security Policy*. New York, 1982.

George, Alexander, and Richard Smoke. *Deterrence and American Foreign Policy*. New York, 1974.

Gilpin, Robert. *American Scientists and Nuclear Weapons Policy*. Princeton, 1962.

Green, Phillip. *Deadly Logic: The Theory of Nuclear Deterrence*. Columbus, Ohio, 1966.

Harvard Nuclear Study Group. *Living with Nuclear Weapons*. Cambridge, 1983.

Herken, Gregg. *The Winning Weapon: The Atomic Bomb in the Cold War, 1945–1950*. New York, 1980.

———. *The Counsels of War*. New York, 1985.

Hoopes, Townsend. *The Devil and John Foster Dulles*. Boston, 1973.

Kahn, Herman. *On Escalation: Metaphors and Scenarios*. New York, 1965.

———. *On Thermonuclear War*. 2d ed. Princeton, N.J., 1960.

———. *Thinking About the Unthinkable*. New York, 1962.

Kaplan, Fred. *The Wizards of Armageddon*. New York, 1983.

Krepon, Michael. *Strategic Stalemate: Nuclear Weapons and Arms Control in American Politics*. London, 1984.

McNamara, Robert. *The Essence of Security: Reflections in Office*. New York, 1968.

Mandelbaum, Michael. *The Nuclear Question: The United States and Nuclear Weapons, 1946–1976*. New York, 1979.

Martin, Lawrence, ed. *Strategic Thought in the Nuclear Age*. Baltimore, 1979.

Quester, George. *Nuclear Diplomacy: The First Twenty-five Years*. New York, 1970.

Rosenberg, David. "American Atomic Strategy and the Hydrogen Bomb Decision." *Journal of American History*, LXVI (June, 1979), 62–87.

————. "The Origins of Overkill: Nuclear Weapons and American Strategy, 1945–1960." *International Security*, VII (Spring, 1983), 3–71.

Russett, Bruce. *The Prisoners of Insecurity: Nuclear Deterrence, the Arms Race, and Arms Control*. San Francisco, 1983.

Sherwin, Martin. *A World Destroyed: The Atomic Bomb and the Grand Alliance*. New York, 1975.

Smith, Alice K. *A Peril and a Hope: The Scientists' Movement in America, 1945–1947*. Chicago, 1965.

Smith, Gerard. *Doubletalk: The Story of the First Strategic Arms Limitations Talks*. New York, 1980.

Tonelson, Alan. "Nitze's World." *Foreign Policy*, XXXV (Summer, 1979), 74–90.

Wohlsetter, Albert. "Bishops, Statesmen, and Other Strategists on the Bombing of Innocents." *Commentary*, LXXV (June, 1983), 15–35.

CRITICAL WORKS ON THE ETHICAL DIMENSIONS OF AMERICAN
FOREIGN POLICY

Cohen, Marshall. "Moral Skepticism and International Relations." *Philosophy and Public Affairs*, XIII (Fall, 1984), 299–346.

————, et al. *War and Moral Responsibility*. Princeton, 1974.

Ford, Harold, and Francis Winters, eds. *Ethics and National Security*. New York, 1977.

Frankel, Charles. "Morality and U.S. Foreign Policy." *Worldview*, XVIII (June, 1975), 13–23.

Held, Virginia, et al. *Philosophy, Morality, and International Affairs*. New York, 1972.

Hunt, Michael. *Ideology and U.S. Foreign Policy*. New Haven, 1986.

Johnson, James T. *Can Modern War Be Just?* New Haven, 1984.

————. *Just War Tradition and the Restraint of War*. Princeton, 1981.

MacIssac, David. *Strategic Bombing in World War II: The Story of the United States Strategic Bombing Survey*. New York, 1976.

National Conference of Catholic Bishops. *The Challenge of Peace*. Washington, D.C., 1983.

Nye, Joseph. *Nuclear Ethics*. New York, 1986.

Paskins, Barrie, and Michael Dockrill. *The Ethics of War*. Minneapolis, 1979.

Selected Bibliography

Ramsey, Paul. *The Just War: Force and Political Responsibility.* New York, 1963.
——. *The Limits of Nuclear War.* New York, 1963.
——. *War and the Christian Conscience.* Durham, 1961.
Rappaport, Anatol. *Strategy and Conscience.* New York, 1964.
Russett, Bruce. "Ethics of Nuclear Deterrence." *International Security,* VIII (Spring, 1984), 36–54.
Schaffer, Ronald. *Wings of Judgment: American Bombing in World War II.* New York, 1985.
Sellers, James. *Public Ethics: American Morals and Manners.* New York, 1970.
Sullivan, William. *Reconstructing Public Philosophy.* Berkeley, 1982.
Thompson, Kenneth W. *Morality and Foreign Policy.* Baton Rouge, 1980.
——. *Moralism and Morality in Politics and Diplomacy.* Lanham, Md., 1985.
Tucker, Robert. *The Purposes of American Power: An Essay on National Security.* New York, 1981.
Walzer, Michael. "Political Action: The Problem of Dirty Hands." *Philosophy and Public Affairs,* II (Winter, 1973), 160–80.
——. *Just and Unjust Wars: A Moral Argument with Historical Illustrations.* New York, 1977.
Werell, Kenneth. "The Strategic Bombing of Germany in World War II." *Journal of American History,* LXXIII (December, 1986), 702–13.

Index

Index

Index

153, 169, 170–71; on "scientific mind," 155–56; on modern culture, 162–63, 166–68

Mugwumps, 57

Nagasaki: bombing of, 66, 79, 80, 81, 82, 86, 87

National Endowment for Democracy, xii

NATO, xv, 31, 39

Natural law, 51–52, 55

Neorealism, 173–74

New Feudalism, 135, 136

New Left, 136

New pacificism, 103

New Republic, 20

Nicaragua, xii

Niebuhr, Reinhold, 7, 16; "pessimistic-optimist," 7–8; as realist, 12; biography of, 16–19; on Christian realism, 16–19, 55; on moral rhetoric, 17–18; on U.S. as superpower, 38; his Hegelianism, 55; on original sin, 55; on philosophy and public affairs, 55–56; on ideals and self-interests, 63; on the use of force, 68–70, 76–80; on nuclear testing, 112; on competence and democracy, 143–44, 147–48; on domestic weakness, 154; on modern culture, 160–61

Nitze, Paul, 74, 83, 88; on use of force, 86–87

"No first use," 164

Nonproliferation treaty (1968), 112, 119

Normative limitations, 2, 3, 5, 8, 18, 61, 75–76, 95, 173

NSC-68, pp. 28, 87, 89

Nuremberg and war crime trials, 46, 96; bombing of, 66

Obliteration bombing, 72

One Worlders, 32

One World or None: Lippmann's contribution to, 93–97

Open Door policy, 26

Oppenheimer, J. Robert, 83, 88, 89, 93, 94

Pacificism, 32, 67, 68

Panama, xii

Parrington, Vernon L,. 57

Pearl Harbor, 67

Pells, Richard H., 58

Percy, Charles, 115

Plato, 121

Pluralism, 51–52, 56–61

Precision bombing, 73, 76–77

Prudence, 32, 64, 50; as principle of realism, 5–6, 32

Raison d'etat, 45–47, 64

Rationalism, 3–4, 5, 11, 18–19, 32, 51–52, 162, 163, 166

Reagan Doctrine, xii

Religious faith, 172; of Morgenthau, 13; of Neibuhr, 16–17; of Lippmann, 20

Responsibility: ethic of, 43–46, 63, 175–76

Roosevelt, Franklin D., 74

Roosevelt, Theodore, 139

Rotterdam: bombing of, 66

Santayana, George, 20

Schlesinger, Arthur M., Jr., 60

SDI (Strategic Defense Initiative), 114

Singal, Daniel J., 58–59

Smith, Gerard C., 117

Smith, Michael J., xvii, xviii

Sovereignty: and supranational structures, 94–97

Sputnik, 105, 107

nann • dean acheson • hans morgenthau • george
einhold niebuhr • walter lippmann • dean acheson
enthau • george kennan • reinhold niebuhr • walte
an acheson • hans morgenthau • george kennan
uhr • walter lippmann • dean acheson • hans mor
orge kennan • reinhold niebuhr • walter lippmann
on • hans morgenthau • george kennan • reinhold
lter lippmann • dean acheson • hans morgenthau
nan • reinhold niebuhr • walter lippmann • dean a
s morgenthau • george kennan • reinhold niebuhr
nann • dean acheson • hans morgenthau • george